child of wonder

Praise for *Child of Wonder*

"When it comes to nurturing creativity in children, this book has it all: encouragement and inspiration, quick tips and ideas, and detailed instructions for parents who think they are creatively challenged. And the best news is that the steps that help children develop creatively are exactly the same steps that help them develop cognitively and emotionally."

—Lawrence J. Cohen, Ph.D., author of *Playful Parenting*

"*Child of Wonder* is the operation manual that every child wishes her parents would read. And parents will be glad they did, for here they will find a wealth of ideas for turning every day materials and experiences into the extraordinary, sparked by the child's imagination."

—Hilary Flower, author of *Adventures in Gentle Discipline*,
La Leche League International

"Ginger Carlson skillfully demonstrates that the things we need to inspire our children are within ourselves and our homes. Her love of wonder is infectious and her prescription for nurturing children is both creative and practical."

—Josh Golin, Associate Director,
Campaign for a Commercial-Free Childhood

"*Child of Wonder* considers the whole child in its approach to education, offering activities easily adapted to a wide variety of learning styles. Children are encouraged to run and climb and jump and explore, as well as to read and write and draw and sing... Ginger is a clear-sighted, realistic visionary."

—from the Foreword by Melissa Hart,
Professor, University of Oregon, educational writer,
and award winning author of *101 Ways to Love a Book*

"This delightful and useful book is a joyous antidote to the canned electronic amusements which stifle our kids' creative juices. Parents and teachers who explore its wealth of ideas will benefit themselves, their children, and the future potential of our society."
—Jane M. Healy, Ph.D.,
    Educational psychologist and author of *Your Child's Growing Mind: Brain Development and Learning from Birth to Adolescence*

"Truly a thoughtful and engaging resource for families...creative thinking and creative play all in one."
—Sandra Kauten, Editor *Oregon Family*

"What you are holding in your hands—*Child of Wonder*—is a must-read for all parents and early childhood educators who care about how to raise thoughtful young ones. Ginger Carlson offers a multi-facetted, thought-provoking approach to nurturing natural instincts of our children. It will help us raise caring, curious, and creative kids; ready for whatever challenges their lives might offer them."
—Arun Toké, Editor *Skipping Stones* Magazine

cHiLd of WoNder

Nurturing Creative & Naturally Curious Children

by

Ginger Carlson, M.A. Ed.

Common Ground Press

Child of Wonder: Nurturing Creative and Naturally Curious Children
by Ginger Carlson, M.A. Ed.

Common Ground Press
Post Office Box 51274
Eugene, Oregon 97405 USA
htttp://www.commongroundpress.com

ISBN: 978-0-9797027-0-9; 0-9797027-0-4
Library of Congress Control Number: 2007904706

Publisher's Cataloging-in-Publication Data

    Carlson, Ginger.
       Child of wonder : nurturing creative and naturally
    curious children / by Ginger Carlson.
       p. cm.
       Includes bibliographical references and index.
       LCCN 2007904706
       ISBN-13: 978-0-9797027-0-9
       ISBN-10: 0-9797027-0-4

       1. Creative ability in children. 2. Parenting.
    I. Title.

    BF723.C7C37 2007   153.3'5
                      QBI07-600196

FOR ZEAL

who keeps me in a perpetual state of wonder!

coNteNts

Part I: To Nurture the Creative Child

*The Mindset and Environment
for Creativity and Thinking*

Part 2: Ways of Play

Encouraging Imagination, Curiosity, and Confidence Through Play, Experimentation, and Discovery

Part 3: Explore More

Developing Creativity and Thinking Skills Through the Arts, Sciences, Stories, and Media

Acknowledgments

Enormous awe-inspired and loving gratitude to:

The children of the Sparkly Starflies, who keep effortlessly listening. And to all the other children in my life, especially Ian, Montana, Hailey, Papaya, and, of course, Zeal, who have provided me such an up close and personal view of true creative wonder!

Special appreciation to the many parents, grandparents, educators, and children who have graciously shared their ideas, insights, experience, and lessons of life and learning; I could not have written this book without their input.

To my *Wonder Wise* and *Wondershop* column readers, for reading and for keeping me writing, and especially for all your kind comments and thoughtful questions over the years. To Candace Hunter for thoughtful attention to detail. To Joe Freedman for insightful, wonder-full design.

To my friends, colleagues, and personal teachers who have supported me in one way or another through the writing and production of this book:

Amy Costales, Amy Samson, Amy Pritchard, Julie Jackson, and Leoni Daniels: Thank you for your valuable feedback, from the early idea stages to the many drafts of this manuscript. Amy Hopkins and Darlene Muller of Bikram Yoga College of India in Eugene, Oregon, as well as the other wonderful Bikram Yoga studios where I practice when I travel: thank you for keeping me strong, flexible, determined, patient and clear in spirit, mind, and body. June Cotner, for your valuable feedback about my book proposal. Thank you to the entire Youth Services department of the Eugene Public Library, especially Jeff Defty, for conversation, insight, and dedication to children. Melissa Hart, thank you for your ongoing support, and for writing the Foreword for this book. You continually inspire me. Elisabeth Harrod, I value your parenting, your professional input, your contributions to this book, and most of all your friendship. Great appreciation to Kelsey Nava-Costales, photographer extraordinaire and Wondergirl Grace! To the most phenomenal J'Nelle and Stephen Holland, Daryl and Penny Harris, Rob Foltz and Leauriy Polk: thank you for your enduring friendship, inspiration, and support in all creative ventures! Jennefer Harper, for all you do for this world, thank you for your honesty, your feedback, your partnership, and your friendship. Civilizania awaits!

Finally, I am grateful to my entire family, most notably my brother Alex, my sister Julie, and my parents, Bill and Sherri Carlson, for encouraging me to find my own way, supporting my choices, and unconditionally loving.

And the most wondrous thanks of all to my husband and partner in parenting and life, Raphael, who always makes time to read what I write, asks the questions that make me think, loves and supports with everything he has, and simultaneously holds my hand while holding up the ceiling.

WHat i HaVe LearNed

Dear Fellow Parents and Other Facilitators of Learning,

Children are creative by nature, yet scores of materials exist for adults who want to tap into and recapture their creative sides. So somewhere between childhood and adulthood, we, one way or another, lose contact with that true nature. Well, welcome (or welcome back) to wonder!

Child of Wonder began taking on this concrete form in a small café in Santa Monica, California in the early nineteen-nineties. As an elementary school teacher, my world revolved around how I could create an environment for my students that would both honor and develop their thinking and self-expression. A decade and three continents later, my life was still joyously centered on discovering, creating, and wondering. Then, becoming a parent myself, my mission was brought even further into focus. It has become a labor of love and, more than that, a way of life. But to say that it started over a cup of coffee would be gravely underestimating the truth.

Much of what I am and the way I approach life and learning is directly related to the way I was parented as a young child. I believe, as many researchers do, that I am not an exception. As parents, we have the greatest impact on our children's desire to learn and ability to express themselves.

When I was a child, the poem *Children Learn What They Live* by Dorothy Law Nolte hung in our hallway. I walked past it thousands of times. Occasionally, I would pause in my day and stop to read and reread all it had to say. As I grew, I processed and internalized all a child could learn if treated the way he or she deserved: patience, confidence, faith, justice, appreciation, and ultimately, to find love in the world. Now, as an adult, I am recalling memories and assessing what I have learned by what I have lived.

I have learned that stacking wood is easier and faster if we do it together. I have learned that skinned knees and concussions heal, but riding on handlebars is probably not the best idea; there are better ways to learn balance. I have learned that you should still turn the water on, just check for scorpions before you stick your hand in the hole. I have learned that math is less daunting and much more fun if you are learning about it while sitting on Dad's lap; even engineering can be approached like an art. I have learned that the best mess is the one you make when decorating cookies your own way while listening to Mom tell tales about playing King of the Mountain in the backyard of the little white house on Castle Street. I have learned that sitting around the dinner table is my favorite place. We will never all agree on how to live, but it is much more peaceful and fulfilling to listen to the point of view on the other side of the table than to try to prove you are right. After all, a game of dominoes is so much better when we are all laughing. I have learned that every stumbling block is a lesson. Sometimes the sudden change in perspective is what helps us move forward. I have learned that learning is a lifelong journey.

Thank you for taking the step towards living a life of creative wonderment with your children. I am honored to continue the journey and the learning with you.

Happy discovering, creating, and wondering!

—Ginger Carlson, M.A. Ed.

Lyrics by Harry Chapin

flowers are red

The little boy went [to his] first day of school
He got some crayons and started to draw
He put colors all over the paper
For colors was what he saw
And the teacher said. . .
What you doin' young man?
I'm paintin' flowers he said
She said... It's not the time for art young man
And anyway flowers are green and red
There's a time for everything young man
And a way it should be done
You have got to show concern for everyone else
For you're not the only one

And she said...
Flowers are red young man
Green leaves are green
There's no need to see flowers any other way
Than the way they always have been seen

But the little boy said...
There are so many colors in the rainbow
So many colors in the morning sun
So many colors in the flower and I see every one

Well the teacher said. . .You're sassy
There's ways that things should be
And you'll paint flowers the way they are
So repeat after me. . . .

And she said. . . . Flowers are red young man
Green leaves are green
There's no need to see flowers any other way
Than the way they always have been seen

But the little boy said again. . . .
There are so many colors in the rainbow
So many colors in the morning sun
So many colors in the flower and I see every one

Well, the teacher put him in a corner
She said. . . It's for your own good. . .
And you won't come out 'til you get it right
And are responding like you should
Well finally he got lonely
Frightened thoughts filled his head
And he went up to that teacher
And this is what he said. . . and he said

Flowers are red, and green leaves are green
There's no need to see flowers any other way
Than the way they always have been seen

Time went by like it always does
And they moved to another town
And the little boy went to another school
And this is what he found

The teacher there was smilin'
She said...Painting should be fun
And there are so many colors in a flower
So let's use every one

But that little boy painted flowers
In neat rows of green and red
And when the teacher asked him why
This is what he said. . . and he said

Flowers are red, and green leaves are green
There's no need to see flowers any other way
Than the way they always have been seen.

But there still must be a way
to have our children say. . .

There are so many colors in the rainbow
So many colors in the morning sun
So many colors in the flower and I see every one

foreword

I met Ginger Carlson first as a parent. She lived with her husband and their young son, Zeal, across the street from me. As I worked from home on my latest textbook for young readers, I listened, enthralled, to conversations between mother and child. "Why is Cody named Cody?" Zeal might ask, spotting my Sheltie in the front yard. This would elicit a question from Ginger, seemingly casual, but deliberately designed to foster critical thinking skills in the mind of her three-year-old son. "Why is Zeal named Zeal?"

Why indeed? Answering such a question with another question asks the child to contemplate not only the origin of a name, but the meaning and applicability of a word. In this case, Zeal is aptly named—with Ginger's gentle guidance, he approaches the world with absolute delight. Together, they turn a neighbor's birthday into an exciting lesson in cooking, artwork, generosity, and timing so that the homemade pancakes are warm and the paint on the birthday card is dry just as the honored one awakes and discovers the gift of a breakfast in bed.

A short while after meeting Ginger and her family, I became aware of her as an educational consultant. She offers intelligent personal guidance to parents and children who balk at the borders of traditional K-8 education. Parents frustrated by the limitations of crowded classrooms in public schools come to her for suggestions on how to develop lesson plans based on their child's real-life experiences. Under her tutelage, they learn how to integrate critical thinking and creativity into their child's basic daily tasks and personal interests. A unit on owls becomes an opportunity for a field trip to the local raptor center, in order to study the birds up close. Violin lessons take on new meaning during free noontime concerts at the performing arts center downtown.

Parents and teachers hope to instill children with a lifelong love of learning. In this technological age, however, we find ourselves easily overwhelmed with computers, videogames, television, and all those temptations which distract us from a deep appreciation for the natural world and all that it has to teach us. As Richard Louv points out in his *Last Child in the Woods: Saving Our Children from Nature-Deficit Disorder*, our children show an increasing tendency to view nature as more of an abstraction than a reality. The activities in *Child of Wonder* bring nature back into focus. Maple seed pods become fascinating lessons on aerodynamics, seed dispersal, and horticulture. The tired, overused sandbox gives way to gardens and bird feeders and sidewalk art, resulting in minds that open and expand and create marvels equal to all that they've discovered around them.

But Ginger is a clear-sighted, realistic visionary; she advocates a balance of nature and technology, and embraces a multitude of educational possibilities offered by responsible use of computers and the Internet. The book devotes considerable time to the roles that technology and the media can play in the education of young people, offering applicable websites, discussions on how to create media, and how to use critical thinking skills in order to achieve media literacy.

As a longtime educator for a K-12 independent study program, I often field questions from parents concerned about their child's lack of motivation for a static curriculum. "I want my children to have the opportunity to do creative projects as part of their education, but I'm not sure how to go about designing them," parents tell me. *Child of Wonder* provides parents with an abundance of suggestions for projects that nurture a child's inherent interests. In user-friendly format, with inspiring examples and anecdotes, Ginger encourages parents and teachers alike to see education not as a duty, but as pure pleasure.

Clear directions, supported by theoretical discussions, allow readers a range of options. Adults pressed for time can implement ideas quickly and easily, incorporating teachable moments into everyday activities. Alternatively, parents and teachers with more time to devote to a child's education can delve deeply into the book, studying the pedagogy that informs each chapter, and using the activities as a jumping-off point to design entire creative curriculums.

Over the last few decades, educational theorists have focused on the importance of educating the whole child. Many have focused on learning styles, pointing out that people learn in a variety of ways. One student may learn best by hearing instructions, while another achieves success with a more tactile, hands-on approach. *Child of Wonder* considers the whole child in its approach to education, offering activities easily adapted to a wide variety of learning styles. Children are encouraged to run and climb and jump and explore, as well as to read and write and draw and sing. The book pays special attention to how we, as adults, must care for our young people—chapters on the importance of "Yes Days" and the creation of private creative spaces remind readers that we all, regardless of age, respond best to positive feedback and respect for our individuality and personal space.

When last I saw Ginger and her son Zeal, they sat reading about dogs in a large, comfortable chair at a local bookstore. Once again, I heard him ask a question—this time, about the book in his hands. Ginger replied with a question seemingly spontaneous, but designed in an instant to nurture creative thought. Zeal answered his question and hers with peals of delighted laughter. I watched a moment more—the enthusiastic young boy and his mother—and thought of how readers of *Child of Wonder* will discover their own zeal in the possibilities for an education based on creativity and regard for the world in all its wonder.

I knew Ginger Carlson first as a parent. Now I, along with countless readers, rejoice in knowing her as an insightful and dedicated educational writer.

—Melissa Hart, M.F.A.
Professor, University of Oregon, educational writer, and
award-winning author of *101 Ways to Love a Book*

to Nurture the creative child

The Mindset and Environment for Creativity and Thinking

I happened to be here
a leaf among days & when mornings fall
awaken I happen to hear

chapter 1

explore your wonder

Understanding and Encouraging Creativity

*"Do you hear it?" A young boy looked up at his mother with
wide eyes.
"Hear what?" his mother asked.
"My heart," he said. "It's whispering!"
"What is it saying, honey?"
"It says. . ." He listened for a moment, "It says. . . keep listening."*

From the moment they enter this world, children are keen
observers. With each observation, they bring a unique interpreta-
tion and expression. They are special individuals with their own
views and ideas. They bring a passion to life at which many adults
marvel. If given freedom, they play, experiment, question, make
enormous messes, take risks, explore freely, and then apply what
they have learned to the world by thinking, reporting, solving
problems, expressing ideas, shouting, crying, laughing, and creating anew. Somewhere along the way, the driving force for that
freedom of expression, listening to the heart, begins to fade.

As children grow and enter situations where they must con-
form for issues of safety and, sometimes, adult sanity, they often
become more limited in their expression. "What happened to our

baby who used to make up songs on her way to Lompaland?" asks one couple, reminiscing about the change they notice in their daughter as she has grown and become more practical. With an increased need to look to others for direction and approval, children often create less imaginatively and sometimes even lose the ability to think for themselves and solve problems effectively.

By stimulating thought, honoring the creative process, and offering ways of unique expression, parents can help their children return to the place of listening with more understanding, knowledge, and abilities than ever before. Towards that end, we must first look at what really is this elusive thing called creativity.

DEFINING CREATIVITY

The creative personality is certainly a complex one. The definition of creativity varies, depending on with whom you talk. One accepted definition is that creativity is a new idea brought to fruition by a unique listener. Ancient rhetoricians described it as invention. Creativity has also been described as the ability to create ideas and solve problems. It can be seeing the same thing as everybody else, but seeing it differently. Creativity can be taking a challenge and innovating on what has already been done.

Nurturing creativity is a means to extend problem solving and positive change well past childhood. Mihaly Csikszentmihaly, one of the foremost creativity researchers, said it is a "more personal experience, which affects the way one experiences life, with originality, openness, and freshness." He speaks of one type of creativity with a lowercase "c" and another type with a capital "C." He states creativity (with a lowercase c) "makes life enjoyable," while Creativity (with a capital C) "changes culture." If joy is an indication of creative expression, we only need to look to the smiles that appear as children play to witness creativity. If life is enjoyable, then how can it not change culture if even only on the smallest of levels? Perhaps "creativity" has the great potential to *grow up* into "Creativity."

This process of growth is what we can help children tap into and continue to nimbly grasp throughout life. We live in a result-oriented society. The process of discovery and play has often held less value than the end product, perhaps because children have

not always been allowed to be children. The notion of "childhood" is a relatively new phenomenon in the last one hundred years. With increasing perspective of what a child deserves to experience in childhood, we now suddenly find ourselves in an exciting place where we can help guide thinkers who enjoy life and, ultimately, develop the problem solving skills and ingenuity to make the changes they envision as they become adults. As children are still able to effortlessly listen to the whispers, it is essential that we nurture that ability to keep hearing how the heart wants to express itself. In doing so, the world and its possibilities will be endless for our children.

ENCOURAGING CREATIVITY IN THE HOME

Aristotle offered a definition of creativity, which eventually became the accepted definition for rhetoric, as the "art of discovering the available means of persuasion for any given case." He described the art of this discovery as being systematic. He suggested looking only to the commonplace ("topoi" to the Ancient Greeks) to realize and discover creativity. What is more commonplace than the home?

When babies arrive, no one can tell parents how these distinguished visitors will change their lives. Children often become their parents' greatest teachers. They challenge and change parents' thinking. In this book, we will ask questions, explore ideas, dialogue about what creativity means in the commonplace of young children, and consider how we might assist these teachers on their creative journey.

Parents as Creative Guides

Parenting styles have surely arisen in the search for what makes creative families and what kind of parents the most creative peo-

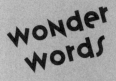
ple have had. Almost without exception, parents who provided materials and resources that encourage growth of imagination have raised those who have developed their creativity to the fullest. They allowed creative expression and encouraged discourse. They held high standards of behavior, but were not heavy handed with rules.

Parenting styles are as diverse as people, so there is certainly no single right way to raise a creative and critical thinking child. However, there are specific actions parents can take to encourage creative thinking in the home. The following are foundational beginnings that parents can incorporate to encourage creativity in the home. Each of these topics will be revisited throughout the book with specific ways for incorporating each key point of a creative life into daily routines and learning experiences. As you learn about these elements of creativity, consider how they might fit into your own parenting style and the needs of your family.

Encourage Self-Reliance

Being able to solve problems and thinking creatively do not happen on their own. They also do not happen without encouragement along the way. Eventually, it is the ability to create and solve problems with a degree of individuality that leads to the Creativity we strive towards. William Blake said, "No bird soars too high, if he soars with his own wings." We can help our young children discover those wings by giving them responsibility and freedom to try things on their own: tying shoes, experimenting in the kitchen, packing their own snack, pouring their own milk even if it spills, or choosing their own combination of clothes for the day. This is not to say that if your child has been characterized as clingy that he or she cannot be creative. It is important to recognize every child as having a unique starting place, and some children will need extra support towards getting to a place of self-reliance. Equally important is to recognize that a child who feels secure in his or her relationship and attached to his or her primary caregivers will be more apt to take risks and experiment with independence.

Creativity by Association

Just like other personality traits that can "rub off" on a child, creativity can be enhanced through association. Surround yourself and your kids with other creative people you know. Let them experience the varied ways other people in their lives use ideas and solve problems. From the neighbor mechanic figuring out how to make the old lemon run again to making cookies with only a few ingredients, talk to your children about how solutions are found to everyday problems. Help children witness examples of creative thinking by experiencing local artists, filmmakers, musicians, scientists, writers, storytellers, or other creative people who would otherwise not be in your social or professional circles.

Play with Your Imagination

Rudolf Steiner asserted, similar to Jean Piaget, that imagination is one of the stages of development. A creative climate, one that has a true relationship with creative behavior and imagination, is one in which humor and play are active and evident. Play with puzzles, brainteasers, simulations, games, and toys that allow for creative expression. Be silly. Laugh. Have fun!

Provide Creative Space

Provide a stimulating environment. Some kids can handle more stimulation than others. Know your kids, and their personal thresholds for activity and stimulation, and go from there. Most importantly, balance your supplies and creative space. If there is too much going on or supplies cannot be found, creativity can be inhibited. Overabundance of things and stimulation has led to thrill seeking rather than children having a genuine desire for creative problem solving. Find the balance between excess and having just enough to stimulate creativity.

Creativity Busters

There are many obstacles that inhibit creativity from developing. If we can understand these creativity busters, we can avoid them. Do your best to avoid these obstacles to creativity:

Competition

The most creative influential people have many times had the dubious role of being the firstborn. It is likely this has been the case because the firstborn becomes the child who carries responsibilities and by virtue of birth order, becomes more independent. Children, especially second, third or fourth children, can oftentimes feel in competition with other siblings. This can inhibit creativity, especially if final products are viewed competitively over process. Provide opportunities for the child to shine on his or her own. Take a *Yes Day* (Chapter 6) or set a *date night* where your child can connect with you one on one and share ideas and wonderings about the world.

Dictator Mentality

Studies about businesses and corporations have found that employees create more and think better when they feel they are on a more even playing field with their boss, when their feelings and opinions matter and are taken seriously, and when they feel appreciated for their hard work. While we don't want to treat our families as corporate entities, the same translates to a family. A study of the family life of people who both resisted and followed Adolf Hitler in Nazi Germany found that those that succumbed to the ideas were raised in households where rules were steadfast and harsh. Those who resisted came from families who valued respectful argumentation.

Thinking You are Not Creative

While creativity has its traits and a recognized skill set that has been developed and refined by many influential people around the globe, there has never been clear evidence that creativity or the ability to be creative is an inherited trait. Nor is it reserved for a small group of artists. Creative people come from all walks of life. They come from all social and economic classes, and from all sizes of families. Creativity is an individual matter. It is available to all people.

Criticism

Nothing will stop a child from creating or thinking imaginatively more effectively than someone they love and respect telling them "No," or "Don't!", that they are doing it wrong, or they are not good enough. Keep in mind: every negative statement requires seven positives to balance out its effect on self-esteem.

Popular Culture

While popular culture, its art and music, can be very creative, it can also be a creativity inhibitor if it means that children are primarily being guided by toys bearing the likeness of certain characters from television and movies. Take time away from the ads, character of the day, and other popular items. Doing so will provide you respite and mental space to think outside those pop items.

Stress

When a child worries about anything other than being a child, they are going to feel stress. Stress is not altogether a bad thing and can be a motivational factor. However, stress is also a response to conflict or change. Stress for a child can come from anything: a change in schedules, starting school, a new sibling, being punished, a family's financial problems, a death in the family, arguments with friends, moving, separation, or divorce. Recognize how stress manifests itself in your children: bedwetting, nightmares, tension with friends, withdrawal, fearfulness, crying, rocking, overeating, or not wanting to eat at all. Once you have recognized sources and manifestations of stress, you can help a child cope with it by reading picture books which deal with the issue, role playing with puppets and dolls, providing many opportunities for physical activity to release stress, and talking honestly about concerns and family matters. Releasing points of stress in a child's life can do wonders for their ability to problem solve and think creatively.

Step Outside of Your Comfort Zone

Routines are important for children. The predictability of a day is calming and can ease transitions. That said, it is only by experiencing new ideas and having ideas challenged that creativity can continue to develop. Question your habits and then provide your children with new ways to look at the world. Travel. Encourage cultural pursuits. Read together about topics you normally don't choose. Try something new.

Allow for Quiet Time and Relaxation

The brain needs quiet time to solve problems. Without relaxation, the human being does not have mental space to create or innovate. If you must, schedule quiet time. Write stay at home days into your calendar and stick to them. Take a few moments of down time. Just like having a baby, there is no "perfect" time. There will always be something to do, somewhere to be. When you choose quiet time, you choose time for creativity to flourish.

Use Responsibilities to Your Advantage

There is nothing that you cannot be creative with. Use your daily responsibilities (laundry, cooking, cleaning, gardening, pet care, etc.) to both model and help your children practice being creative. Approaching daily tasks as practice in creativity will also make them more fun and easier, even more so when they are done together. As Carol Channing said on the *Free to Be You and Me*

album, "To seem sunny as summer weather, make sure, when there's housework to do, that you do it together!"

Provide Examples of Creativity

Albert Einstein said, "Setting an example is not the main means of influencing others; it is the only means." Creativity is available everyday if we can listen for it. A model of creativity can be a child watching her mother using a recipe as a guideline and making it suit the needs of their family. It can be telling stories that show another person being creative. It can be the extra flair, a fancy scarf or a unique belt, added to an outfit. Find everyday creativity and just listen to it. In addition, expose children to other impressive examples of creativity. Incredible buildings. Wondrous works of art. Opera. Ballet. The examples are endless.

Make Mistakes

"Only those who dare to fail greatly can ever achieve greatly."

—Robert Kennedy

Scientists and inventors find solutions, make discoveries, and experience breakthroughs by having to try and try again. Encouraging creativity in no way means needing to do things perfectly or the *right way* all the time. Delight in the mistakes you and your children make. Model viewing each stumbling block as a learning opportunity with the potential to lead to the solution or perhaps something completely different.

Marcel Proust said, "The real voyage of discovery consists not in seeing new landscapes but in having new eyes." Perhaps he should have also mentioned having new ears. Listen to your heart whisper. Keep listening. It's telling you to explore your wonder.

Picture Books that Provide Examples of Creativity

And to Think That I Saw it on Mulberry Street by Dr. Suess

The Big Orange Splot by Daniel Manus Pinkwater

The Dot by Peter Reynolds

Encyclopedia Brown by Donald Sobol

Frederick by Leo Lionni

If... by Sarah Perry

Ish by Peter Reynolds

Jillian Jiggs by Phoebe Gilman

The Little Prince by Antoine De Saint-Exupery

Miss Rumphius by Barabara Cooney

The Lion and the Little Red Bird by Elisa Klevin

The Magic Tree House series by Mary Pope-Osbourne

The Maggie B. by Irene Haas

Mud is Cake by Pam Munoz Ryan

Oh, Were They Ever Happy! by Peter Spier

Purple, Green and Yellow by Robert Munsch

Roxaboxen by Alice McLerran

Sky Castle by Sandra Hanken

Terry's Creature by Deborah Gould

Unicorn Dreams by Dyan Sheldon

Weslandia by Paul Fleischman

chapter 2

Let the flower bloom

Allowing Children to Arrive at Their Own Pace

A flower is a delicate creature. From seed, the journey requires special care and extreme patience. Balance the nutrients in the soil. Prune just so. Take care to water, but not too much. Clear the weeds. Allow sunshine to reach it regularly. Leave it alone. Eventually the bud appears, begins to open, and the vague scent of the blossom reaches the nose.

Children too, need this time to find their blooming potential. Characteristics of creative individuals who have been studied had common threads running through their households. A common key component of the house in which a creative individual was reared, is that children were allowed to become independent. Their mothers were often present, and facilitated their needs, but were not overprotective. Their originality and pace was respected.

When our children are born, we often see a blank slate rich with potential. Parents bring high expectations to the new experience of being a parent. Many people spend a great deal of time telling children to *act their age* and otherwise forcing age and development expectations upon them.

In schools, benchmarks and standards are the measure for whether a child is learning at a pace that has been previously determined. Many of the brightest, most curious, and creative students do not meet this measure because tests take only facts, and not potential, into account when assessing.

Learning happens on a range, on a continuum. Among many educational professionals who agree that children develop best at their own pace was Maria Montessori. She believed in helping children reach their fullest potential by creating a climate and community of learners that were multi-aged, so no child felt either ahead or behind. She stressed the importance of allowing children to develop at their own unique pace.

LETTING THE FLOWER BLOOM

The potential of the flower is greater when we allow it to bloom before reaching out to pick it. Holding back from the urge to pick is easier if we understand the elements of allowing children to arrive at their own pace.

Understand the Range

Over the years, childcare and health professionals have developed a timeline for how children develop: walking will happen at around a year, talking starts to emerge anywhere from several months to well past the first year, a child will naturally learn to read between ages four and ten. It is important to know the milestones of development, but also that children learn and grow at their own pace. It is also important to know that children who reach certain milestones early are not necessarily healthier or smarter or better than those who achieve them later. The range of what *normal* is can be quite wide, and usually balances out with time.

Careful Observation

If we understand our children's strengths and challenges, likes and dislikes, personality traits, preferences, and the intimate details of their learning styles (see sidebar in Chapter 3, *Breaking Ground*), we hold the key which unlocks their innate ability to thrive. In order to understand how our own children fit into the model, we must first spend time carefully observing them.

One mother recalled how her daughter who eventually went on

to become a member of a diving team and lifeguard and found much joy in the water, sat on the edge of the swimming pool for the entire first session of her early childhood swimming lessons. "She didn't want to get her *babysuit* wet," the mother recalls. "I told the instructor that's how she is and that she will get in when she is ready." Sure enough, the second session proved to be fruitful. "She jumped right in and started swimming. She'd been paying close attention, but needed space before she felt comfortable in trying."

Some children jump right in and some sit on the edge of the pool for weeks before dipping their toes in the water. Both are valid forms of learning. As parents, the more we are able to observe our children and how they react to situations, the more we will be able to support them in their creative ventures.

Provide Access

As parents, one of our hopes is to raise children that are *well-rounded*. Naturally, human beings have varied interests. While many children naturally focus on a few specific areas such as trains or dinosaurs for a period of time, it is important for parents to try to balance and provide access to all areas of interests.

Stephen Wosniak, one of the founders of Apple Computer Company, is just such an example. He showed an interest and strength in both math and electronics. At the time, schools in his area would not allow students to take both academic and trade classes. His parents believed strongly in allowing him access to whatever his interests were. They challenged the district policies, and he was the first student to be able to break those boundaries to enter the courses of his own choosing. The background in both disciplines was what led to his future success in developing Apple's ground-breaking operating system.

"Are you sure Leo's a Bloomer?" asked Leo's Father.
"Patience," said Leo's Mother.
　　　　　—from *Leo the Late Bloomer* by Robert Kraus

Disequilibrium

Philosopher and developmental psychologist Jean Piaget described the stages of child development to be on a pendulum. Children, because they grow so quickly, will go from being in a state of balance to a state of disequilibrium and back again. One parent described the phenomenon as the "half-birthday-out-of-whack-zone." About every six months she noticed a shift in her son and things were just difficult during those periods. He was taking in so much information and growing so rapidly, with so many changes, that it was manifesting itself as a struggle socially. Recognizing the pattern was important for his mother's peace of mind and ultimately for the child to work through the pattern on his own and eventually make it back to a steady equilibrium. Learning this was developmentally natural empowered both mother and child.

Value Struggle

Another ingredient that allows children to develop creatively is encouragement to make mistakes. Michael Jordan, in a Nike commercial, said, "I have missed more than 9000 shots in my career. I have lost almost 300 games. On 26 occasions I have been entrusted to take the game winning shot...and missed. And I have failed over and over and over again in my life. And that is why...I succeed."

The only way we can discover our limits and the possibilities for going past them is to test them. Being challenged outside one's comfort zone and still being able to learn at your own pace is certainly a balancing act. Robin, mother of two, recalls when her oldest child, MacKenzie, was five and just beginning to express himself through writing. He decided he detested it because it was a struggle for him. He was a perfectionist and did not like the idea of trial and error. Rather than force him to do it, Robin explored the balance and allowed him space to not have to physically write for a while. A novelist herself, she continued to model writing and the revision process. Pointing out her own struggles, his understanding of what makes success evolved. Eventually, he began to dabble in writing again. Robin proudly reports that his writing is increasingly imaginative!

Once a child has come to solve a problem with support, she will be better equipped to take the process to other areas of life. As we witness individual creative processes, it is important to remain open to the potential of the flower. It will indeed bloom in its own time.

chapter 3

breaking ground

Setting Up and Organizing the Creative Environment

Exploration, n. 1. an act or instance of investigation.
2. the investigation of unknown regions.

Many people keep an image in their minds about the creative artist in her studio with spilled paint cans and missing brushes, or a shaggy-haired mad scientist who works among piles of notes and empty test tubes in cramped quarters. Any person who creates will attest, while in the middle of a project, creative workspaces do surely find themselves in disarray. However, the images we often hold onto about the unorganized, cluttered space is not only an inaccurate picture of artists, but it is also not necessarily best for children as they learn how to explore and think creatively. Organization and structure can provide a place from which creation can bloom.

Exploration is the foundation for developing a creative thinker. Without the investigation into materials, possibilities, and imagination, it is difficult for that creativity to emerge and then fully develop. In order to encourage that exploratory nature in our children, we must first begin with the environment in which our children spend most of their time. "But how do I encourage exploration and still keep the house clean?" one concerned mother asked.

To get the most out of their spaces, children need to know what materials are available to them, be able to find supplies when they want them, and then be able to move freely in their space in order to use them. While creativity is certainly not confined to the home, setting up and organizing your living spaces can be the catalyst for getting creativity started and flowing freely. In this chapter you will find guidelines for organizing, utilizing, exploring, and enjoying your living spaces.

KNOW YOUR SPACES AND THOSE WHO USE THEM

As you begin to set up your environment for learning and exploration, consider what each room of your home offers each creative being who uses it. Draw a map of your home and list the activities that usually occur in each area. What is the intent of each space? What items need to leave the space for the intended action to occur there? What can I add to the space to make it more conducive to reading quietly, painting, exploring with building materials, or making music? If your space is for infants and toddlers, get down on the floor and experience the spaces from their point of view. How easy is it to get to the items you want to play with?

Keep in mind that this creative space does not need to be in just one section of your house. You may have a spot in each room that is set up for different creative uses. For example, you might keep your writing supplies near the kitchen where your child often sits and works while you cook. Or you might have book boxes in several places in the house such as in the living room, in the bedrooms, or even in the bathroom. Assess your home and figure out what kinds of activities usually take place where, or determine in which spaces you would like to encourage a particular type of activity.

If your child has a table at which she enjoys doing craft or art projects, then that would be a logical space to create your art area and displays. If she likes to curl up on a certain set of pillows and read, then keep a basket of reading supplies and books there. If you can have some kind of creative outlet in each space where your child happens to spend time, all the better. Although this seems obvious, often we overlook the act of planting some of these tools that would make life and creativity flow easier.

WORKSPACES

Take your little creator's style into account when you are setting up spaces for them to play and work, which are one in the same at this early stage. Does she need to get up and walk around often? Then think about having two or more workspaces, ones that she can move between for a change of pace and scenery. Does your child need a quiet space away from outside noises (road traffic, etc.) and other distractions (younger siblings, media, or other household activity)? Then you might consider having a special room or corner set up that is a designated *quiet zone*. If distractions are an issue, keep the environment calm by removing items such as activity packed posters, the active family pet, a ticking clock, lights that may buzz, or other items you notice being a distraction.

If space is a premium, consider using a fold out table hooked up to one free wall. The only down side would be that your creator wouldn't be able to work on extended projects such as puzzles that require the table to be "out" for a long time. An obvious plus would be that you can maximize space.

A COLOR OF MY OWN

Using color, either on walls or adding other colored accessories in your home, can provide a soothing, inspiring, or exciting experience, depending on the color. Some colors such as red, purple, yellow, and other bright colors are considered more conducive to creativity than others. Use colors to unify or divide a room. Give new life to a room you want to designate as a special place to work on creative family projects. Start a family mural and don't worry about it not being professionally done. Even consider painting furniture to give it a new look or function. Dweezil Zappa, the eldest son of musician Frank Zappa, remembers one of his fondest childhood memories when his mother and father "painted our kitchen table white and let us decorate it."

If you are in a space that you cannot paint, consider hanging tapestries, colored sheets, or even blank canvases from the wall for your family to decorate.

MARVELOUS MOBILITY

One goal to keep in mind while you are setting up your space is that children should be able to move from one activity to the next, and between rooms with ease and comfort. Look at your pathways and doors. Is there anything blocking your mobility? A mobility rule of thumb is that there should be at least a three-foot distance between items that are in pathways. This not only creates open minds for creativity to happen more often (because the mind is not jumbled with other concerns), but it also allows creativity to emerge in more interesting and varied ways.

SEPARATION OF NOISY AND QUIET AREAS

Using a divider can help create a quiet zone. It can diminish noise level, give privacy, and create a psychological "space" where the child can get into his or her own creative zone. Dividers can be store bought or homemade using string, plastic pipe, or wood and material. If you make it like a curtain, it can easily be pulled back to open up your space when it is not in use.

If your space is small and it is difficult for you to weed out noise, but you have a child who needs to have quiet, incorporate strategies such as offering noise canceling headphones (available anywhere you can buy electronics) for your child to wear when he chooses, which noticeably cut out more than seventy percent of noise. You may also consider adding white noise through the use of a noisy fan, air filter, white noise machine, or a radio between stations quietly humming static.

INDEPENDENCE

Children are naturally dependent on their care-givers, but too much dependence leads to a helplessness that makes it difficult for creativity to bubble to the surface. Since self-reliance is important in the development of a creative spirit, children need to be able to access their creative tools when the spirit catches them. When placing furniture, play items, art supplies, and your children's other creative tools, keep the independence factor in mind. If certain supplies need to be placed out of reach of younger children, consider providing step stools for your older children to get what they need when they need it.

OPEN SPACES

Wide open spaces are especially appealing to children wanting to explore and express themselves. Allow for creative movement, spontaneous moments of creativity, or space that allows for large puzzle working by setting up an open space somewhere in your house. This may mean that you need to remove some furniture or push large pieces up against walls. Consider a throw rug to define a stage or dance area and ground the open space.

MEETING PLACES

While you want to keep in mind that you need open spaces, you also want to make sure you have places for groups to gather for a meeting of the minds. Places where meetings take place should be free of media stimulation such as a television or other items that would be distracting to the meeting process. To make spaces for meeting as a group more comfortable add bean bags, a warm and cozy soft chair, or other chair arrangements that face each other rather than towards a television. See Chapter 5, *The Family Think Tank*, for tips on holding family meetings.

SOFT SPACES

Comfort is an important aspect of living, and especially living creatively. Provide low to the ground, comfortable spaces to work such as pillows and cozy corners with a low table in addition to a proper desk or table where you do projects. Allow your children access to blankets and other soft items so they can create their own cozy spaces.

ORGANIZING THE CREATIVE HOME

As you look at and begin to analyze your spaces, designate areas for special activities, and find places for all the tools needed to accomplish those goals, organization and systems for organization begin to emerge. This section of the chapter will provide ideas for communication systems and exploration center set up and organization.

CREATING A COMMUNICATION SYSTEM

Communication is vital to creativity. Within your creative space it is a good idea to set up some type of communication system. Especially as children become more independent, it is a nice tool to keep the lines of communication open.

Letter Notebooks

When stocking up on supplies during all those back-to-school sales, include a notebook designated for you and your child to write back and forth to each other. Intended to be an on-going activity, a letter notebook develops letter-writing and spelling skills. It is a communication tool that offers a place to practice creative expression.

When your child writes a letter (using her own words, pictures, or prewriting scribbles), be sure to respond on the next page within a few days. Make sure you use your best printing, as opposed to cursive handwriting, so she will be able to attempt to read it on her own and begin to recognize letters and some words. Get as creative with this as possible. Draw pictures, include stickers or add special treasures. Tell her you are proud of her and be specific in your letters. Ask questions and expect an answer to your questions. Have different family members respond as well as encouraging her writing to different family members.

Mailbox

Children love mail, so why not give them their own? Consider setting up a mailbox of sorts somewhere in your house where the letter notebook can be stored and other letters for family members and friends can await delivery.

Allow children the freedom to choose the materials to create a mailbox. Will we use a real metal mailbox? One made from a cardboard box? Perhaps it is a special tray. Will it be decorated with paint, feathers, stickers, or not at all? As letters are written, they can be placed in the mailbox. Put the flag up to indicate a waiting letter.

In-Out Box

Similar to a mailbox, consider an in-out box system in your creative learning space. As projects are completed, they can be moved to the out box to share with parents, or as a system to let everyone know what is waiting for input into the portfolio (see Chapter 22, *The Other Side of the Mountain*, for ideas about creating a portfolio) or for possible entry into your museum. See Chapter 23, *My Treasure House*, for ideas about museum making.

Message Boards

When busy families try to juggle many different schedules, communication is sometimes difficult. A message board (either magnetic, cork, dry erase, or chalk board) in your home for all family members to communicate in their own way can lighten the load, help ease the minds of the parents who need to carry most of the juggling, and inspire creativity. Leave creative notes using special notepaper or Post-it™ notes for each other or simply a word that inspires or makes other family members smile or laugh.

Sign Systems

Open and closed signs around the house (and affiliated with certain activities) can be valuable tools if you want to put limits on what can be done when. Flipping over a sign on the computer, TV, or other high frequency and stimulating areas can be a good form of silent, non-arguable communication. Color-code your signs for early or pre-readers so everyone in the house can be in on the communication system! See Chapter 20, *Words My Way*, for other sign ideas.

SETTING UP EXPLORATION CENTERS

While it is on the rare occasion that a child will investigate into the depths of a closet or take something off a high shelf, there is definitely something to be said for the saying *out of sight, out of mind*. When setting up your exploration centers, keep this in mind. The more you can keep these items visible and easily stumbled upon, the more exploration will actually take place.

POSSIBILITIES FOR EXPLORATION

When it comes to open exploration of materials, the possibilities can seem endless and even overwhelming. With a little organization and forethought, the possibilities will seem less daunting. Possible ideas for exploratory materials include:

Natural Materials

Some people call this a Nature Table or Nature Wall. Perhaps it is atop an old electric organ, and goes by the name of Nature Piano. Regardless of where it is or what you call it, set up an area in the house that can collect treasures from the outdoors. Another great way to store objects from nature (pine cones, bark, moss, shells, stones, tree branch "blocks") is a basket that can easily be carted from one area of the house to another. Just keeping those natural objects easily available will encourage exploration with them. "Wow, Mom! Look what happens when I roll these chestnuts across the floor. Let's make a bowling game out of them!"

Sewing

Besides just a fabulous way to work on fine motor skills, sewing (on fabric or even just cardboard with holes) and other types of handwork are great ways for a child to express himself or herself creatively. Use an embroidery hoop or an old frame to create a practice sewing space. Sew on special pictures, twigs, leaves, or other special finds from a nature walk. Even make it a guest book where friends, family members, and visitors can "sign" their names.

Tactile Exploration

Allow your child to use a different part of her brain by creating a place for tactile exploration called a feely box. Use a shoebox or wood to make a box with a hole on one side that is big enough that you can place a few mystery items within it, and cover them in cloth. Each week, place new items for feeling and discovering such as simple household items like a screw or tape dispenser, or items you have collected on your nature table. Attached to the wall in a fairly prominent place, this can be a great opportunity for the whole family to get in on the exploration and the conversations.

Cooking

Few will dispute the various ways cooking can add to a child's life and learning, but few also regularly allow creative exploration in the kitchen. Consider giving your kids their own space for mixing and baking, real and imaginatively, while you are working on supper. If there is not enough room in your kitchen to set up an entire play kitchen for your children, give them a shelf or cabinet of their own. For more ideas for getting kids creatively involved in cooking, see Chapter 13, *Thinking Outside the Recipe*.

Carpentry

Don't be afraid to allow your child to go beyond pounding out the little pegs in a play cobbler's bench or using plastic hammers. Exploration with real building materials like sandpaper, screwdriver, hammer, and nails can help children, among other things, build confidence and creativity. Rather than using a kit to build a birdhouse or what not, let them explore with how things go together. Provide bits of wood, nails and screws, and other creative building materials (perhaps piping insulation, bamboo pieces, or pieces of bendable materials such as wire) and be open to an interesting new tunnel for the train set, a bed for Zippy the Lion, or even an abstract sculpture.

Building Materials

Get wild and crazy! Mix and match. Explore with everything you can to build the towers in your mind. Try these and add a few of your own:

- maple blocks
- cut up pieces of branches and tree bark
- Legos™
- K'nex™
- Brio MEC™
- dominos
- cards
- cd or tape cases
- stones
- sugar cubes
- books
- pillows
- shoe boxes
- blankets

Exploratory Items

Wondering what to do with all those random pieces of ribbon, Velcro, or corrugated cardboard? Start a collection of all the misplaced items in your home and create your own exploration box where you can touch, smell, observe, and maybe even taste their unique properties. Different from a feely box, this allows you to use all of your senses to explore. Throw in a magnifying glass for continued exploration. Use the exploration box to talk about textures and functions. Let the pieces guide you in creative art exploration or new inventions.

Dress Up Center

A few simple costumes can completely change the direction of your child's creative play. See Chapter 9, *To Pirate Ships and Castle Moats,* for information about a dress up center in your home.

Set-Up and Organizing Tips

- Start slowly. Don't try to organize your house or set up creative centers all in one day.

- Make a plan.

- Find a place for everything. Whether they are organized into bins, bags, boxes, or on shelves, designate an organization system for toys and playthings.

- Do it together. If your children are involved in the organization and the ideas for where to put things and how to organize comes from them, they will be more likely to help keep it organized.

- Accept mess. Recognize when your child is creating and allow disorder during those moments.

- Hold a family clean up time. Consider setting aside 15 minutes a day, perhaps after dinner or before bedtime, when everyone in the family helps to put away and organize the day's tools. Make it a game by using a timer, singing a song, or seeing who can pick up the magic toy that one person in the family has designated so. How wonderful to start the next day with a clean slate.

Music and Movement

There is a proven profound connection between movement and learning. Movement can both stimulate and calm the brain, priming it for the introduction of new knowledge. Add to that connection the child's birthright to experience and make music and you have the perfect combination. Let your children learn and actively teach themselves by providing ample opportunities for them to listen, chant, move in different ways, and make music with their bodies, voices, and outside instrumentation. Keep a box or shelf visible with instruments and other movement props so it can happen whenever your child gets the urge. See Chapter 15, *Jump, Jiggle, Jive,* and Chapter 16, *Music in Me, Me, Mee!,* for suggested movement and music activities.

Mirrors

Mirrors allow a child exploration of his own body as he uses them to peer at his teeth, check out an elbow, or see the back of his knee. Separate from growing concerns about young children already focusing on self-image, mirrors can be used as an exploration tool rather than to judge appearance. See Chapter 17, *Everyday Math Magic*, for ideas about using mirrors as an exploratory and pattern making tool.

You may possibly have finger or hand puppets. Many parents report having these items, but that they fail to find uses for them. Add a simple hole to your ready or homemade puppet theatre and then place a mirror on the opposite side of the theatre so your puppeteers can see themselves while they are working on a show. It will certainly add a new dimension to their storytelling and puppetry if they can see the movement of the puppets.

Science

Science is anything you are investigating! Set up a science tub, bucket, corner, bench, or table. Experiments can happen during the little lulls in the day when your child pauses briefly and looks around for what to do next. Get messy and make mistakes with magnets, food coloring, light and sound, things that float and sink, flight, senses, or states of matter. Since the possibilities with science are so vast, try picking just one topic a month and rotating what lands on your science table. This, as opposed to changing it weekly or putting out too much at one time, will encourage deeper exploration with each set of materials and is likely to mean less parent-activity coordinator-burnout. See Chapter 18, *Lightbulb Moments*, for more ideas about exploring science concepts creatively.

Travel Box

Being on the go, in the car or in a bike trailer, can sometimes be monotonous for children. Provide a basket, box, or bag with exploratory items to take along on simple outings or long trips. Possible on-the-go items include: a magnifying glass, binoculars, a simple fold out telescope, magnets and magnetic objects, a small jar of dough or modeling clay, a harmonica, colored pencils or crayons, a small pad of paper, silly putty, travel bingo cards with items your child might see on the road, and a kaleidoscope. If you can, also consider keeping a tray in your car or bike trailer to provide a usable work space while you are on the go.

So here you go! Explore your world, your wonder, and your home! Investigate the unknown regions of the mind, creativity and all the treasures hidden in your closets, bookcases, and cupboards. Most of all, have fun!

Consider Your Child's Learning Style

Children learn in different ways. If we are able to understand the individual learning needs of our children, we can then create opportunities for them to thrive in their absorption of information and creative expression. When setting up your home environment, ask yourself the following questions and make careful observations about how your child learns best. Finding the answers to these questions will give you insight to how you may wish to set up your home environment to best meet the needs of your child.

• Does my child prefer to hear a story, see a movie, or play outside?

• Does my child prefer to listen to music, read a book, or take a walk?

• Does my child prefer to listen to music or a book on tape, watch television, or play a game?

• Is the best way for my child to remember to repeat a concept or words over and over to herself, make a picture in her head, or just do it?

• My child understands instructions better when...someone explains them to him, he can read them or see pictures, or someone shows him how?

• When my child is thinking...she talks to herself, sees pictures in her head, or needs to move around?

• Does my child learn best when it is quiet, noisy (like cars or street noise), with music playing, or people talking?

- Does my child do best sitting at a desk or table, sitting on the floor, lying on the bed, floor or couch, or at a tall table?

- Does my child do best with bright light, low light, light coming in from a window, or direct sunlight?

- Does my child get hot or cold easily?

- How often does my child need to eat?

- What are my child's most and least favorite colors?

- What time of day does my child feel most active?

- What time of day does my child seem to have low energy?

Adapted from the Modality and Environment Assessments from *Discover Your Child's Learning Style,* by M. Willis and V. K. Hodson, copyright 1999, included with permission from the authors, www.learningsuccesscoach.com.

Consider Multiple Intelligences

Howard Gardner, renowned Harvard professor and researcher, developed the Theory of Multiple Intelligences which asserts that people are naturally intelligent in many different areas, not just those assessed in traditional ways.

Use the checklists on the following pages, developed by Thomas Armstrong, Ph.D., to consider your child's natural intelligences when setting up your home environment. Your child may show one dominant area of intelligence or overlap in several areas.

Characteristics of Linguistic-Verbal Intelligence

_____ writes better than average

_____ spins tall tales or tells jokes and stories

_____ has a good memory for names, places, dates, or trivia

_____ enjoys word games

_____ enjoys reading books

_____ spells words accurately (preschool: does developmental spelling that is advanced for age)

_____ appreciates nonsense rhymes, puns, tongue twisters, etc.

_____ enjoys listening to the spoken word (stories, commentary on the radio, talking, books)

_____ has a good vocabulary for age

_____ communicates to others in a highly verbal way

Other Linguistic-Verbal Strengths:

Logical-Mathematical Intelligence

_____ asks a lot of questions about how things work

_____ computes arithmetic problems in his or her head quickly (preschool: math concepts are advanced for age)

_____ enjoys math class (preschool: enjoys counting and doing other things with numbers)

_____ finds math computer games interesting (no exposure to computers: enjoys other math or counting games)

_____ enjoys playing chess, checkers, or other strategy games (preschool: board games requiring counting squares)

_____ enjoys working on logic puzzles or brain teasers (preschool: enjoys hearing logical nonsense such as in *Alice's Adventures in Wonderland*)

_____ enjoys putting things in categories or hierarchies

_____ likes to experiment in a way that shows higher order cognitive thinking processes

_____ thinks on a more abstract or conceptual level than peers

_____ has a good sense of cause-effect for age

Other Logical-Mathematical Strengths:

Spatial Intelligence

_____ reports clear visual images

_____ reads maps, charts, and diagrams more easily than text (preschool: enjoys visuals more than text)

_____ daydreams more than peers

_____ enjoys art activities

_____ draws figures that are advanced for age

_____ likes to view movies, slides, or other visual presentations

_____ enjoys doing puzzles, mazes, _Where's Waldo?_ or similar visual activities

_____ builds interesting three-dimensional constructions for age (e.g., LEGO™ buildings)

_____ gets more out of pictures than words while reading

_____ doodles on workbooks, worksheets, or other materials

Other Spatial Strengths:

Bodily-Kinesthetic Intelligence

_____ excels in one or more sports (preschool: shows physical prowess advanced for age)

_____ moves, twitches, taps, or fidgets while seated for a long time in one spot

_____ cleverly mimics other people's gestures or mannerisms

_____ loves to take things apart and put them back together again

_____ puts his or her hands all over something he or she has just seen

_____ enjoys running, jumping, wrestling, or similar activities (older: shows this in a more "restrained" way, e.g., woodworking, sewing, mechanics) or good fine-motor coordination in other ways

_____ has a dramatic way of expressing himself or herself

_____ reports different physical sensations while thinking or working

_____ enjoys working with clay or other tactile experiences (e.g., finger-painting)

Other Bodily-Kinesthetic Strengths:

Musical Intelligence

_____ tells you when music sounds off-key or disturbing in some other way

_____ remembers melodies of songs

_____ has a good singing voice

_____ plays a musical instrument or sings in choir or other group (preschool: enjoys playing percussion instruments and/or singing in a group)

_____ has a rhythmic way of speaking and/or moving

_____ unconsciously hums to himself or herself

_____ taps rhythmically on the table or desk as he or she works

_____ sensitive to environmental noises (e.g., rain on the roof)

Other Musical Strengths:

Interpersonal Intelligence

_____ enjoys socializing with peers

_____ seems to be a natural leader

_____ gives advice to friends who have problems

_____ seems to be street smart

_____ belongs to clubs, committees, or other group organizations (preschool: seems to be part of a general education social group)

_____ enjoys informally teaching other kids

_____ likes to play games with other kids

_____ has two or more close friends

_____ has a good sense of empathy or concern for others

_____ others seek out his or her empathy or concern for others

_____ others seek out his or her company

Other Interpersonal Strengths:

Intrapersonal Intelligence

_____ displays a sense of independence or a strong will

_____ has a realistic sense of his or her strengths and weaknesses

_____ does well when left alone or to play or study
_____ marches to the beat of a different drummer in his or her style of living and learning
_____ has an interest or hobby that he or she doesn't talk much about
_____ has a good sense of self-direction
_____ prefers working alone to working with others
_____ accurately expresses how he or she is feeling
_____ is able to learn from his or her failures and successes in life
_____ has high self-esteem

Other Intrapersonal Strengths:

Naturalistic Intelligence

_____ talks a lot about favorite pets or preferred spots in nature
_____ likes field trips in nature, to the zoo, or to a natural history museum
_____ shows sensitivity to natural formations (e.g., while walking outside, will notice mountains, clouds; or if in an urban environment, may show this ability in sensitivity to popular culture "formations" such as sneakers or automobile styles)
_____ likes to water and tend to plants
_____ likes to hang around the gerbil cage, the aquarium, or the terrarium
_____ gets excited when studying about ecology, nature, plants, or animals
_____ speaks out for the rights of animals or the preservation of planet earth
_____ enjoys doing nature projects, such as bird watching, butterfly or insect collections, tree study, or raising animals
_____ brings to school bugs, flowers, leaves, or other natural things to share with classmates or teachers
_____ does well in topics that involve living systems (e.g., biological topics in science, environmental issues in social studies)

Other Naturalist Abilities:

Checklist from _Multiple Intelligences in the Classroom_ by Thomas Armstrong, Ph.D., reprinted with permission from the author.

chapter 4
the art of questioning

Asking the Right Question at the Right Time

"What do you notice about that dinosaur's mouth?" Sharon asked her son Alex, who like many four year-olds has a penchant for pre-historic creatures. He responded enthusiastically, "Look at his sharp teef, Mom! I think that long one was for tearing the meat off his prey!" He leaped to the floor pretending to be a meat eater. His confidence in his own ability to draw conclusions soars, something that may not have happened had he been posed the question in a less open way.

Sharon knew that Alex, a dino enthusiast, would easily be able to rattle off which dinosaurs were meat eaters and which were not. But instead of just drilling him with "Do you think that dinosaur is a meat eater?" she decided to take the conversation (and the thinking) further.

WHAT'S IN A QUESTION?

We often ask questions to get our children to prove what they know or have just done or to spit out *the facts*. If words alone have so much power, forming them into the right question can move mountains, the kind that make for more creative and confident thinkers.

With a good question, we have the power to focus our children's attention, help them observe and compare their surroundings, to pose problems, investigate relationships, and stimulate their reasoning. At the same time, we can also establish an atmosphere of trust and provide intriguing experiences, which guide their curiosity.

Testing knowledge, we commonly ask factual questions of our children. With these types of questions, only one answer is usually possible. The child answers the question and considers himself done. In order to begin children thinking more divergently, consider asking more interpretive questions. These are questions that have more than one answer, yet are still supported with the evidence your child draws from experience and their own research of the world. Interpretive questions build on one another and offer children opportunities to think about the bigger picture.

A LOADED QUESTION

At the heart of asking good questions is a true exploration of our children's wonderings about life. Through our use of questions we can help them tap into their creativity by allowing them to have a truly inquiry-based learning experience, driven by their own interests, observations, and predictions. Instead of asking yes or no questions or ones that require them to simply state the obvious, offering instead questions like "What happens if…?," "Can you find a way to…?," or "I wonder what would happen if…" can open conversations which may lead to exciting places.

When we ask evaluative questions, we are more truly exploring our children's opinions about the world. We are asking for a point of view or belief and in this way, there are no wrong answers.

"When children are asked questions in an inquiry-based way, it affects how they approach future problems," said Dr. Mark Hertle, Senior Program Office for Precollege Science Education at Howard Hughes Medical Institute. "They look at things and search for how best to pry out the answer. They become the adults who are experimenting with new recipes and constantly learning new things."

BEYOND THE RIGHT ANSWER

While we may ask the right question, equally important for our children's development is accepting their answers. Giving your child a chance to explain herself more fully, without judgment or constant correction, will be a key component in gaining confidence in her own learning and exploration.

As parents, it is sometimes hard to be able to accept that the right answer is not always the one we were looking for. When questions are truly spontaneous and natural and have elicited a thoughtful conclusion (even if it wasn't what we would consider right), instead of correcting their observation, we can simply respond with "That's really interesting; I hadn't thought of that," or "Thank you. I understand." A simple acknowledgment can be all children really need to further their thinking. Too much correcting of children's thinking causes them to lose confidence in their own wonderings and conclusions about the world.

ANSWERING QUESTIONS WITH QUESTIONS

During the first half of the 5th century, Socrates walked the streets of Athens talking to the people he met, from slaves to common people to other philosophers of his time. He did not discriminate because he felt he could learn as much from a slave as he could from a king.

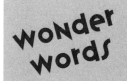
wonder words

"The important thing is not to stop questioning."
—Albert Einstein

Socrates' mother was a midwife. While she did not actually give birth, she helped guide mothers through that process which their bodies already knew how to do. Socrates likened his work to hers. He felt he could help people "give birth" to the ideas in their heads and guide them towards their own insights, since real understanding comes from within.

Towards this end, Socrates developed his art of discourse by continually asking questions, which led people to uncover their own thinking. Answering questions with a question has since come to be known as the Socratic Method. By offering specific and logically leading questions in response to questions your child asks, you present your child an occasion to experience the joy and excitement of discovering ideas on his or her own. It is an opportunity to provide constant feedback while highlighting specific areas where a child may have misunderstood something, allowing her to make her own discoveries. Most of all, the Socratic Method arouses curiosity and thinking and provides parents and children an opportunity to learn from each other.

TIME TO THINK

We know that human beings of all ages need space. Without it, our minds are unable to process the large amounts of stimuli and information we expect them to. People think at different rates. So it is important to allow children "think time" when you pose a question. More important than providing an answer to your question is the child's process for coming up with how they want to respond. Think time can be a few seconds or even days of thinking before a child has something to add.

The process of questioning can begin with simple observations, something we tend to lose the ability to do as we move through any given fast-paced day. While on a walk, point out seemingly

The Question Game

This game is a fun way to practice asking open-ended questions! Try modeling it with another adult or older children so younger children will understand how to play.

What you need:

At least two brains

How to play:

Decide on a topic to question.

One person asks an open-ended question; then, like word association, the other person responds with a related open-ended question. Continue for as long as you can without making a statement or repeating a previous question. This can be difficult at first because sometimes you want to give an answer instead of a question. With practice, the questions get funnier and will have children rolling on the floor.

For example, the topic might be a puddle you just jumped in.

Player 1: How do puddles form?

Player 2: Can we use puddles for something?

Player 1: Could crocodiles live in a puddle?

Player 2: If a crocodile lived in this puddle, where would he sleep?

Player 1: What would happen if the crocodile wanted to come in for dinner?

Player 2: Can crocodiles spend time indoors?

simple things you notice and listen to the observations of your child. "Look at the sky. It looks striped today!" "Watch that ant floating on that leaf in the middle of this puddle."

From this place of observation, questions are likely to emerge.

THE BALANCING ACT

As a parent looking to "seize teachable moments," it's easy to go overboard in the question asking department. We want our kids to be thoughtful but may end up overloading them with "What did you build?," "What are you cooking?," or "Can you tell me about your drawing?" So as not to overwhelm your learners or put words in their mouths, try varying questions with statements about what you observe them doing, allowing space for them to elaborate where they feel comfortable. Say things like "What an interesting structure you have constructed," "I see you have been working in your kitchen," or "What a wonderful use of color!"

Learning to ask questions is in fact an art. Bringing thoughtfulness to this art, we can help nurture our children's creativity and allow critical thinking to bubble to the surface. After all, in the words of the poet E.E. Cummings, "Always the more beautiful answer who asks the more beautiful question."

chapter 5

the family as a think tank

A Place for Creative Thinking

In the mind or the heart, on the front porch, in the margins of a piece of scratch paper, or perhaps even in the shadows on the wall just after "lights out": where does creative thinking happen? All those places and more.

In Byrd Baylor's picture book *The Table Where Rich People Sit*, we meet a family who thinks together creatively at the kitchen table. Mountain Girl has called a family meeting, and the subject is money. She says, with much distress, that their family doesn't "have enough of it." Together, they decide to write down all they own. The list grows, but it doesn't look like we would expect. The family soon comes to realize they don't just get paid in money, but with sunsets, the howling of coyotes, and the changing color of the shadows on the mountainside. After much dialogue, they eventually decide that if all the leaders of the world could sit around an old beat up table and share a plate of cookies, there would be less conflict and more harmony in the world.

Harmony: that special place many families strive to unearth to work together to achieve common goals, from who takes out the trash without grumbling, to putting a puzzle together and learning about how the sound comes out of the radio, to even bigger

"A problem well stated is a problem half solved."

—John Dewey

questions like how to fit five growing people into three small bedrooms.

Finding a place where ideas culminate is a creative process in itself that begins the journey towards a more fulfilled and imaginative life. Ideas change the family, and in turn, they change the world. But, as much as we like to think that they just come to us, ideas, creativity, and critical thinking don't just happen on their own. First, a secure foundational structure needs to be set for ideas to come to fruition. The ability to problem-solve, to approach ideas and realize one's unbounded self, lies within a structure of organized freedom. Developing that organized freedom is a step towards living a creative life. Taking a look at the structure we are setting up is the first baby step.

A FAMILY THINK TANK

A *think tank* by definition is an organized group that performs interdisciplinary research. Thinks tanks have left a lasting impression on public policy over the last hundred years. From The Bureau of Industrial Research to The Carnegie Endowment for International Peace (1910) varied examples exist of group members bringing their own specific talents and focus to a common goal, to discuss, debate, explore ideas, and make change.

Setting the stage for creativity as a family unit can look like a think tank, an organized group of family members who work together to create a center where imagination, problem solving, and thinking can happen.

We all love those light bulb moments, the times it seems to just click for our kids. With a family think tank, we can encourage a safe environment where those creative moments can happen more often.

VALUABLE INTERDISCIPLINARY MEMBERS

The original think tanks were unique establishments by today's standards. The primary focus remained on improving and rationalizing the decision making process, regardless of individual belief systems. By recognizing the value each unique mind brought to the process, they managed to steer clear of political agendas. Ideas were born out of true exploration and deep conversation.

As we think of our families as think tanks who share a common goal, we too recognize each member as a valuable piece of the think tank puzzle. View each family member as an expert. Let them play that role; over time their full potential will develop. We may have our communicators, secretaries, financial advisors, time keepers, or facilitators. As a group working together, investigate your family dynamics and the strengths that each person can bring to your creative table. See if you have an expert in discovery, or an expert in asking "why?" How about an expert in movement who can lead your active break times, or an expert experimenter in the kitchen who would like to tickle your taste buds?

While it is easy to sometimes slip into labels, celebrate these roles instead. Let your experts teach the others. As your family experiments and shares together, the roles are likely to change over time. Allow each family member to explore with what they feel comfortable. From this place, they will have the confidence to then venture outside their comfort zone to develop another skill over time.

FINDING SOLUTIONS TOGETHER

Members of think tanks are the technological, social, and scientific problem solvers of the world and could not do so without being able to access their creativity and think "outside the box" together. They are able to discover solutions because, as the old adage goes, *two heads are better than one*.

Practically, even when we value group communication, it can be a struggle for families to put two or more heads together. Decide on a respectful and equal way everyone can be heard, perhaps through the use of a talking feather. Provide set and predictable times where members can check in. During these times, ideas can be discussed, discoveries can happen, and solutions can be found together.

GETTING IN THE GROOVE

If you have ever listened to the dissonant noise coming from an orchestra as it warms up to play, and then heard the perfect sound come together at the raising of the baton, you know what it means to be in accord with each other. You may have even felt it in your own family.

In many families, this is a constant pendulum, going through times of being out of sync and then back in sync with each other and each other's needs. "There are times when we are, as a family, just in a groove," said Karen, mother of four, "and I have to just sit down, accept it for what it is, and be thankful."

When you are in that groove, recognize it, listen to the sweet music, and know that the more you practice thinking together on a shared project or question, the more often you will be able to play together this way.

For the times when you feel out of "the groove" also try to recognize it as a temporary state of being and know that the pendulum will swing the other way soon. Recognize that, as the saying goes, you cannot force a square peg into a round hole. Just like adults, children go through stages with interests, behavior, and attention. Remember: you can't force a flower.

LOOK BEYOND RESPONSIBILITIES

Let's be practical. Sometimes we don't take time to think creatively together because there are just too many tasks that need to get done. Andrew Carnegie and Robert Brookings, founders of two of the oldest American think tanks, believed strongly that by establishing an environment where its members would "not be distracted by...responsibilities," they would then be able to focus entirely on their role as problem solvers and policy makers.

This is not to say that helping your children develop their creative selves more fully means that they can just put responsibilities aside. However, try to look for ways to incorporate saying yes

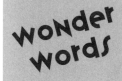

"The most beautiful thing we can experience is the mysterious."
—Albert Einstein

to creativity above sweeping the floor. It can be very difficult to temporarily let go of schedules and mental to-do lists. See Chapter 6, *Yes Days*, for a deeper look in moving towards creativity while juggling daily responsibilities.

SIMPLY PUZZLED

Noam Chomsky said, "Discovery is based on the ability to be puzzled by simple things." A common thread among people who have been described as creative is that they all love what they do. Creative people enjoy discovery and enjoy being simply puzzled.

Children naturally take delight in the simple things in life. As parents, we can continue that natural sense of wonder by appreciating our children's delight. See Chapter 24, *Reach for the Moon, Catch the Stars*, for more about appreciating creativity.

In our family think tanks, being puzzled together and enjoying the discovery that leads to new ideas and solutions is the goal. Perhaps even explicitly, place this as a priority in your family think tank. If at all practical, schedule times to explore together. In our family, this has developed into a once a month Cabin Night when our home becomes a cabin in the woods; we gather together to play games, sing songs, work on projects, and connect with each other by candlelight. However you decide to do it, make a conscious effort to model wondering about things such as the inner workings of the telephone or incorporate a small daily brainteaser. Set up a family puzzle or gather together to discuss something a family member wonders about. Laugh heartily and appreciate your discovery together.

THE AUDIENCE

Not every show needs a standing ovation, but being shown appreciation is a key factor in developing the confidence that makes for more creative thinking.

Find ways to record your family's thinking moments so they don't get lost in what can sometimes seem like a dense forest. Utilize journals or scrapbooks, something that can tell your family's story. Make a family web page or audio archives of special moments. Keep a special portfolio, box, or chest with evidence of your family's creative ventures.

See Part 4: *The Ongoing Journey*, for more ideas on celebrating creativity.

HABITS

Habits are funny things. They are often used to describe being "stuck in a rut" or that they somehow inhibit creativity. Quite to the contrary, creative people have habits, things they do regularly, routines they follow, and ways of being that contribute to their creativity. Developing *habits of creativity*, in the family or personally, is an ongoing practice that involves a state of mind.

Define and develop your family's creative habits together. Focus attention on developing curiosity, spending time together, creating win-win situations for all family members, and appreciating the habits you are developing. Re-examine and refine those habits from time to time.

Holding a Family Think Tank Meeting

Set Regular Times for Meetings

Regular meeting times offer a predictable routine for all family members. Decide on your intervals together: weekly, bimonthly, or monthly. Schedule them on the calendar and remember that "90 percent of success is showing up."

Attendance

In a Family Think Tank, everyone's opinion and point of view is valued and valuable. Meet at times that work for everyone in the family so all voices can be heard.

Keep an Agenda

During the week or month before a meeting, start an agenda. Keep it in a place where anyone in the family can add to it either in pictures or words, perhaps on the refrigerator, family calendar, or some other accessible location.

Open and Close Meetings with a Ritual

Every time you join together as a group, begin and end your meetings with a ritual of some sort. Pass around a plate of cookies, share something you learned since the last meeting, sing a song together, light a candle, or have a group hug.

Model Respect and Cooperation

Human beings learn by example. By modeling a high degree of respect, children will learn to be respectful in return.

Decide on Rules Together

How you run your meetings will be unique to your family structure. Keep in mind that if you come to agreement about what bylaws or rules everyone should follow, and everyone has a say in those rules or agreements, you will be more likely to be able to enforce them. Discuss the difference between a democracy (where family members vote to make decisions) and consensus (where decisions are made only if *everyone* agrees).

Plan Fun Activities

Family meetings don't need to be all about business. With regularity, you will likely find that your meetings don't need to be filled with family problem solving and logistics, but can instead give a focus to working on those exciting ideas, or projects such as volcano making or fun filled outings.

IDEAS CHANGE THE WORLD

As your family's ideas are expressed and solutions are reached, consider the ripples in the family pond and those that reach way beyond it. Watch and know that as your family encounters challenges outside of the home, they will be able to approach them with refined skills and more creativity.

Ideas change the world. Not just the ideas of the major think tanks of the world, but ordinary families thinking extraordinary (and simple) thoughts, with each other in extraordinary ways. If we view our family members as unique thinkers, each with something valuable to offer, we can learn from each other and move towards the solutions that make our families productive, problem solving, and discovering entities. Through this process, we will then find ourselves thinking together at the table where creatively rich and happy families sit.

chapter 6

Creative Days in a World Full of No's and Responsibilities

"This way, Mommy. Do you hear the rocks crunching under my feet?" My son darted past me on the walking trails that wind through the tall evergreens. We spent the morning snooping in the bushes, snacking on only the plumpest berries that practically fall into our palms, and sprinkling fish food (crumbled Autumn leaves) into the creek. This was a *Yes Day*, a day in which I consciously chose to say yes to my child, to honor his spirit, his desires, his choices. There was no "We need to...", "Time to go...", or "One more minute...," and (practically) anything went.

Little fish in a big pond takes on new meaning when you are a parent swimming through each day and trying to get all the things checked off your list. Places to be, things to do, schedules to follow. It can be overwhelming at times. Often, the thing that gets thrown by the wayside is the needs of the child. Not the basic needs, but the underlying intangible needs, the creative spirit of the child.

As parents, our days can often be run by places we *should* be. Many of these places we actually need to be; many are omniscient-parent-have-to's, outings we go on for the benefit of the child: the library, playgroups, music classes, and community activities.

Throughout the day, many parents often find themselves running into power struggles and negative interactions in order to get to the places we feel we should be or do what we want rather than what the child wants. Charles A. Smith, Ph.D., professor at Kansas State University, said, "Although saying *no* tells children what not to do, only by being affirmative do we actually teach them the skills that will be important to them throughout their lives. Learning to make choices (and take responsibility for their consequences) is an important element in developing a courageous spirit and a healthy conscience."

Most parents would agree that we wish our children to grow into adults who are positive and happy. If you have gotten this far in the book, you probably will also agree that we want to engender a love for lifelong learning and creative expression that will follow children beyond their childhood.

In many ways, our daily responsibilities can get in the way of that, but by making more of a commitment towards living in a yes world, living a yes life, and just gathering up little yes moments here and there along the journey, we can use those responsibilities to our advantage, to encourage a more creative, thoughtful child.

Like any ingrained tradition, self-imposed structure is difficult to let go of. However, if our goal is to create confident and creative children who grow into adults who have an impact on our world, we must.

Families can work towards getting past some of these struggles by building connections, directing energy and discipline tactics inward, trying to understand each other better, and having *Yes Days* of their own. Consider the following when planning your own *Yes Days*:

Question Your Agenda

Questioning your agenda can be an extended exercise in being a mindful parent. Getting past reflexively saying "It's time to go," or "One more minute," can be what it takes to create an environment in which we can say yes more often. I've often found myself beginning to enter into a power struggle with my own child as we are getting dressed, getting buckled in, or just plain trying to get out the door in the morning so we can go somewhere that he will enjoy. Imposing an agenda may only instruct him to look to others, rather than himself, for direction. So consider holding a *Yes Day* or yes moment on the spot if there is nowhere you really *have* to be and then pay attention to the quality of each experience as it comes. You may find the world your little one has created with his blocks and trains, and the problem solving and creativity that comes from that, far outweighs the agenda you had in mind.

Listen

Yes Days can give the space and time children need to fully develop into who they will become. When we consciously choose to listen to our children, it provides us the opportunity to stay connected with one another. If your child explains that a mouse lives in every clock turning the clock hands and getting his tail stuck each time it moves (causing the "tick"), consider it an opportunity to gain insight into your child's exploration of the world and how she solves problems rather than correcting her observation, which can often be very difficult for parents who are trying to seize the teachable moments. Remember Socrates?

Honor Sovereignty

Sovereignty is by definition allowing one to gain authority over oneself – a lifelong goal of any whole person. If children live in a world in which they can be confident– one that recognizes their ideas and desires and that these ideas are not "childish", but valuable and valued – then they will become the confident beings we hope for. Children are entitled, like all human beings, to be loved and to find strength in that love. One way we can give them that entitlement is to let them have control over their situations by offering choices.

Childcare advocate and educator Dawn Fry said, "Giving choices is important, because making choices cultivates individuality and self-reliance. Only while making choices can children exercise their human faculties of perception, judgment, discriminative feeling, mental activity and even moral preference. When you offer choices, you are honoring the child's needs and innocence, which ultimately helps them develop self-confidence and build their self-esteem."

Free Yourself From Have-to's

Home is a haven, one in which we can be sheltered from the barrage of outside stimuli. "One of the best ways to have struggle free *Yes Days* is to significantly reduce the child's pressure points—school, fitting in, and adults "nagging" them," said John Bishop, Executive Director of Accent on Success. Give yourself the permission to be free from your busy schedule every now and then. Follow your child's lead and spend the afternoon curled up in bed reading books or cancel your meeting and spend some one on one time sipping cocoa in your pj's. Even turn off the phone for the afternoon. Remember that the world we are creating for our children will directly affect the world they will help create as they grow into thinking adults.

You Can't Please Everyone

If you are parenting multiple children, you surely know that the old adage "you can't please everyone all of the time" rings true. Consider what Michelle and her husband David do every year. While juggling the schedules of their two children, they plan what their family calls *yes trips:* one on one time with mom or dad, without a sibling to compete with. They spend a day doing only what the child wants to do: going to the beach, stopping for a hike or at a lookout on the way, eating when and where their child wants to. Michelle said, "These *Yes Days* have been a reminder that even though we are a unit, we are all individuals and we need to take the time to work on each individual relationship, because the pieces add up to more than the whole."

Families can also set up structures in which to say yes to each child. Take turns on who helps plan dinner. Allow your child to set personal goals for what she will or will not work on for the day. Ask your child his feelings about major changes in the family and appreciate his opinion. Allow children a voice in family decision making.

As we learn to say yes to each other, to the ebb and flow of the world, perhaps these yes days are training for us to live a yes life. Even more so, perhaps our yes lives will be the impression left on our children that in turn creates a yes world. Saying yes, affirming our children as human beings is a gift to everyone. The child is fed by his choices being honored, not having time limits or *have-to's*. Parents are fed by watching the child's pleasure in these simple moments, seeing the world through shared eyes, and breathing in their child's joy.

So go ahead, breathe it in, and say yes to your kids. Create the world you want to see by starting with your own kids and watch the blossoming.

part 2

Ways of Play

Encouraging Imagination, Curiosity, and Confidence Through Play, Experimentation, and Discovery

this brief festival is
not divine but nothing as
precious ever is

chapter 7

WONder tools

Playthings and Toys that Build Creativity

Play is the work of children, and toys are their tools. With so many of these tools gracing the shelves today, it is difficult to choose. Fortunately, for toys to serve their purpose, they don't have to be expensive or store-bought at all. In this chapter, you will find ideas for toys, purchased and homemade, that will help build creativity, imagination, and thinking skills.

BUILDING TOYS

Building blocks are not just a symbol of setting foundations; when a child puts together block structures, they are actually developing pathways in the brain that lead to better reading, concentration, mathematical skills, and critical thinking.

A nice set of maple blocks are not only fun, but worthy in the development of a creatively thinking child. Additionally, Brio MEC™, Legos™, K'nex™, Erector™ sets, pieces of found wood and sticks, boxes and other recycled materials of all shapes and sizes, and even coins or other small stacking objects are all won-

The Wonder of Shadow Play

Shadows have long been weather forecasters, storytellers, weaved into folklore, and a source of good old-fashioned fun. They are at the same time simple, exciting, and ever changing playthings. They require no clean up at all. Best of all, they help us to recognize patterns, think creatively, and use imagination.

Playing with Shadows

As mentioned earlier, a creative climate is one in which humor, play, and discovery are active and evident. Luckily, shadow play is an easy way to help all of those qualities bubble to the surface while encouraging some true critical thinking.

Tell Shadow Stories

With origins in Indonesia and China, shadow puppetry has long been a means of passing down religious and cultural stories and simply having fun. Whether you use a flashlight and your hands, or set up a more elaborate shadow theatre, have fun telling stories with shadows. How many different animals can you make? Can they stick out their tongues? Wag their tails? In what ways can you make them leap, fly, or waddle? Add music for ambience or puppet dancing.

Shadow Time

Before we had Timex, we had shadows. With even small amounts of sun, you too can chart the progress of a day, and even make an accurate timepiece. Begin exploring time with shadows by tracing your shadows with chalk. Come back to the same spot every hour or later in the day to see if your shadow has moved, grown or shrunk, and then discuss why. For the truly scientific, use a Pole-to-Dial converter calculator (available widely on the Internet), which will allow you to customize your sundial to your location for added accuracy.

derful examples of building toys that require and develop planning, critical thinking, problem solving, and imagination.

EXPRESSION TOYS

When children are able to express themselves fully and in a variety of ways, it contributes to added imagination, problem solving, and self-esteem.

Puppets

Use hand, finger, and shadow puppets to tell stories, role play life situations, and even work through fears or concerns that could be causing a child to feel blocked in their ability to communicate. Use a pre-made puppet theatre or make your own from a large box or large piece of cardboard. Consider hanging a piece of material from a doorway with a hole cut from the middle to create a unique and easily stored puppet theatre. Try also hanging a sheet from a desk and shine a light from the back to make a fun shadow puppet theatre.

Musical Instruments

As a means to express oneself, music can be harmonious! Use musical instruments to let children show how they feel or to portray a feeling in a story. Provide or make shakers, drums, and other instruments that will let a child experiment with tone and rhythm. Incorporate harmonicas, bells, whistles, child-sized accordions and harps, blocks covered with sandpaper and recorders for children to hear and make all different types of sounds. See Chapter 16, *The Music in Me, Me, Mee!*, for more information about exploring music.

SIMULATION TOYS

Provide opportunities for children to set up simulations of real life spaces and places, all great avenues for using their creativity and stimulating their imagination by activating prior knowledge and building upon experience. With homemade or store-bought props, set up a post office, restaurant, train depot, grocery store, farmers market, bank, theatre, car wash, parking garage, gas station, department of transportation, or even a lunar landing or space station. Explore lesser known occupations such as shoemaker or tailor through simulation play.

TUB TOYS

Don't just make bath time a time to get in, get clean, and get out. Playing in the bath is a complete sensory experience and is an opportunity to develop understanding of the world and creativity to its fullest, whatever the age.

Make a Shadow Puppet Theatre

1. Drape a sheet over a table or use wax paper to cover a hole in a large box.
2. Trace and cut out desired figures using cardboard or heavy paper.
3. Tape a drinking straw or tongue depressor to the back of your puppets. Use a hole punch and brads if you want your puppets to have moveable parts. Add an extra straw to each moveable part.
4. Use a desk lamp or flashlight to shine light from the back of the sheet or wax paper.

"Children try the world on for size through play. They learn through play and by pretending."
—Raffi

Wonder Words

Float and Sink

Experiment with what floats and sinks. This seems to never go out of style. From empty shampoo bottles and favorite toys to a slew of found objects throughout the house, keep a bag or basket in the tub and guide your child in making predictions about what will float and what will sink. Use fresh or silk flowers, walnut shells, or wood pieces to create boats. Try weaving a few found pieces together to make a raft. To keep the float and sink experiments fresh and exciting, change the items regularly.

Bubbles

Bubbles are perpetually intriguing for people of all ages. Take bubble creativity further by offering the challenge of creating your own unique bubble blowers. Use wire hangers, pipe cleaners, string, straw, plastic containers with the bottoms cut out, or pieces of aluminum foil or plastic wrap. Experiment with how to make extra large or small bubbles. Can you make bubbles inside of bubbles? How about square, triangular, or heart shape bubbles? How about colored bubbles? For strong, long lasting bubbles, try the following recipe:

Magic Bubbles

1/2 cup water

1/4 cup liquid dishwashing soap

  3 teaspoons glycerin or 1/8 cup corn syrup (If you use corn syrup, let it
     sit for a few hours before using it.)

Combine the glycerin and water. Mix them into the dishwashing soap.
Explore!

Favorite Bath Time Stories

Brain Quest Bathtime: 175 Stories, Poems, Questions & Answers, Even Jokes and Riddles, to Read Together With a Little Duck Named Gus by Brain Quest

The Fish is Me!: Bathtime Rhymes by Neil Philip

King Bidgood's in the BathTub by Don and Audrey Wood

Ten Dirty Pigs, Ten Clean Pigs: An Upside-Down, Turn-Around Bathtime Counting Book by Carol Roth

Tub Toys by Terry Miller Shannon

Why is Soap So Slippery? And Other Bathtime Questions by Catherine Ripley

Household Items

Young children are forever interested in the items we use everyday. Plop a few in the bathtub basket and let them experiment with the whisk, egg beater, squeegee, measuring cups, funnel, or turkey baster. If you are uncomfortable with giving up your kitchen tools for such explorations, check garage sales and dollar stores for inexpensive household items.

Tub Paints

Mix equal parts dishwashing liquid or shaving cream with tempera paint for a wonderful, easy-to-wash-off tub (or window) paint. Use sponges, brushes, bath mitts, squeegees, fingers, elbows, or knees to explore on the tub walls.

Special Friends

Turn bath time into creative storytelling time by adding a few favorite puppets or stuffed animals. Don't be afraid. They do dry and may even be extra pleased with the opportunity to get clean along with everyone else.

HOMEMADE TOYS

Experimenting with natural materials can make the best home-made toys. Additionally, items generally thought not to be toys, like rubber bands, boxes, string, tape, sticks, and odd pieces of fabric, have great potential in the world of a child's play.

Dolls

Dolls are perhaps the oldest of toys. Playing with dolls gives both boys and girls opportunity to imaginatively role-play life situations and practice the responsibility of self-care. Use sticks, feathers, flowers, stones, cornhusks, leaves, knobby bits of root, branches, bark, moss, lichen, and vines to make dolls, fairies, or the houses that hold them. Add features to root vegetables (like carrots, beets, turnips, and potatoes) and nuts to make animals. A soft piece of material, perhaps from a worn out baby blanket, can easily be made into a doll. Whether your children play with home-made or store bought dolls, the opportunity to do so is an important one.

Figurines

Use bread dough, clay, marzipan, wire, pipe cleaners, or aluminum foil to make people, animals, superheroes, or replicas of other popular play figurines.

Moving Toys

Toys that move are perpetually interesting. Use straws and disks to make rollers and wheels. Try it on a homemade ramp. Can you make it turn? Cut pieces of cardboard in the shape of a human figure to make a "tumbling man." Can you balance him on a string? Make him jump from one string to the next?

Pulleys

Experiment with pulleys using any number of types of string, yarn, or rope. Pulleys are great for getting special items in and out of bunk beds, lofts, tree houses, or even just up the stairs. Make them go horizontally or on a slope instead of up and down and call it a tram or "people mover." Metal pulley mechanisms are readily available inexpensively at home supply stores, but feel free to go without them as you begin your explorations with pulley systems.

Toss and Catch

Recycle old containers like gallon milk jugs (with a handle are best) to make toss and catch toys. Cut the top off down to where the handle begins. Use beanbags or balls to play "catch" or attach a string to both the handle and the object being tossed to create a solitaire toss and catch game.

HANDWORK

Working with your hands, developing a connection to natural materials, and simply creating from scratch is essential to the development of motor skills and the ability to express oneself. Ultimately, it can be key in the development of an imaginative life. Thankfully, handwork options are plentiful.

Weaving

Weaving, the art of interlacing yarn, thread, or some other form of fiber or natural material, is a wonderful way to combine elements to become a whole. Put together a loom by notching the edges of any size of cardboard to make a doll or kid sized rugs or hangings. Try weaving baskets together from gathered materials on your next walk in the woods. Weave in interesting treasures or beads to make it extra special.

Embroidery

Start even little ones doing handwork with embroidery. Provide any size embroidery hoop and large needles and let them explore. Introduce stitches or pattern ideas only after children have had time to explore with how the needle and embroidery thread work.

Woolwork

Just the feel of wool is enough to connect a child to the natural world and open up the pathways to the soul. With a simple needle and unspun wool, natural or dyed, create flowers, animals, fairies, or other favorite figurines. See handwork resources at the end of this chapter.

Amazing Mazes!

Mazes can be traced back to as early as the 5th century B.C.E. Egypt, with early records placing the Egyptian Labyrinth as more fantastical than even the pyramids. We see mazes appear in literature as early as the Greek myth of the Minotaur. Fortunately for us, our maze journeys will not end with a meeting with the half-man/half-bull creature. Instead, mazes and especially the creation of them, have the potential to lead us to a life of rich creative thought.

The benefits of making and doing mazes are wide reaching. They offer opportunities to practice planning ahead, experience trial and error, and work on motor development, visual tracking, and critical thinking skills. They are engaging and fun for all levels of learners, from toddlers to grandparents, and can be a great point of connection to share ideas, work together, and challenge your thinking-outside-the-box skills.

Webster's tells us that a maze is a confusing, intricate network of winding pathways; specifically with one or more blind alleys. From commercially made mazes to the ones we make ourselves, the opportunity to practice first being confused then working our way through the pathways is a virtually unbeatable way to practice creativity, critical thinking, and problem solving.

Maze Books

Maze books can be found in almost any grocery, dollar, or book store. Keep maze books around (in the bathroom, car, or on the writing table) for your kids to stumble upon. The process of tracing a pencil or marker through the maze can be a wonderful prewriting exercise. For young children just learning to amaze themselves, try *My First Book of Mazes* and *Amazing Mazes*, both by Shinobu Akaishi and Eno Sarris. As children move beyond their first maze books, the selections become more plentiful. Check out *A Super-Sneaky, Double-Crossing, Up, Down, Round & Round Maze Book* by Larry Evans for seasoned mazers.

Maze Games

As far as board games go, there are several good options for all age ranges to have fun with mazes.

Labyrinth™ (and Labyrinth Jr.) by Ravensburger, is probably the best maze game available and has been around for decades in Europe. Rush Hour and River Cross, both by ThinkFun, are wonderful maze type games that involve a good deal of strategy. ThinkFun, www.thinkfun.com, makes junior versions of most of their games but consider just investing in the regular version because they too are leveled and can grow with your kids. Even Candy Land can be revived when you think of it as a maze.

Marble Mazes

Marbles, and their inherent movement, make for great maze travelers. Make your own marble mover by attaching pieces of recycled materials inside a tray or box lid or use pipe insulation to make marbles travel from atop bookshelves or other furniture and do loop de loops. TEDCO makes a particularly wonderful Marbles and Blocks game that offers endless possibilities for marble maze making.

Examples of Mazes

Like all aspects of creative development, provide opportunities to witness maze making. Point out mazes you see everyday in the places you happen to frequent such as the grocery story, your favorite park, a rose or botanical garden, or the local library. One great example of mazes occurring naturally is through up close viewing of an ant farm (available in almost any toy store).

Computer Games and Websites

Many software programs and websites offer interactive maze experiences. They can be fun and challenging, but don't let this be the only mazing you do because computers have yet to offer all the motor skill development and tangible experience that many of the others listed here can.

Make a Maze

Mazes are a great time filler. Make mazes while in restaurants, waiting for a bus, or sitting in the doctor's office. Whether on the back of an old receipt, on a napkin, or in your sketch book, making your own mazes can meet all skill levels and engage all learners. Whether you are working on making them together or challenging each other to finish your creations, incorporate maze making into your waiting repertoire.

For very young children, you can introduce them to mazes by using a Maze Table, the kind with large pieces of wire connected to a table, where you can move a large bead through the maze. Unfortunately, these tables can run up to several hundred dollars. The up side is that a maze like this is not altogether difficult to make on your own. With sculpting wire (available at art supply and craft stores) and a few large beads, you can easily make an ever-changing maze or a more permanent one if it is attached to a table or large piece of wood.

But don't stop there. Real life mazes are the ultimate in maze experiences. Use leaves, sand, snow, pillows, sheets, dominoes, blocks, chalk, hay bales, corn, and even mirrors to make mazes all year long. If you have a small section in your garden that is otherwise not being used, try sprinkling grass or rye seed or red clover in the shape of a small labyrinth. If you have more room, try making a corn maze.

Education and parenting itself is one big maze. We move through each experience trying new directions, sometimes hitting walls or other things that block our way, but eventually we find a way that works for our families. Along the journey, we pick up new techniques, strategies, and ways to think and approach the puzzles life brings. Eventually, we emerge at the finish with a sense of accomplishment and hopefully a few more problem solving skills that will aid us in the next maze we tackle.

Woodwork

Woodwork or carpentry is something completely fascinating to children. It is often shied away from by parents for fear that the child will hurt his or herself, but using real tools is truly a wonderful way for children to develop fine motor skills, hand-eye coordination, and learn to use tools safely. Provide an opportunity to whittle away or build up found or purchased materials. Use real (not plastic) tools like hammer and nails, screwdrivers, sandpaper, and even a bit of supervised sawing for a truly creative experience.

String

While there are many steps that a child can learn to tie and untie various knots, the simple exploration of playing with string can be a valuable step in getting started with handwork. Wrapping string and making loops is the beginning step that develops hand eye coordination, motor skills, and problem solving skills. String can be used creatively by children to make unique opening devices for their doors, pulleys, tie stuffed animals together, make parachutes by tying string to a napkin, or make barriers around play spaces. Just the simple exploration with it provides children an opportunity to make unique creations and find uses for this interesting medium. Eventually, move towards specific knot tying strategies, finger knitting, and string games.

Paper

The art of folding paper is one that requires much thought, concentration, and even skill. Still, even very young children experience success with it. Paper airplanes and origami are wonderful ways to incorporate handwork into the life of a child who otherwise feels discouraged by handwork activities. See the sidebar for resources related to origami and paper airplanes.

NEW AND OLD CLASSICS

Puzzles

Figuring out how things go together is at the heart of solving problems and developing imagination. Some puzzles provide more freedom of expression and different ways to work them than others. Try Pentomino puzzles, Tangrams, block puzzles, Pagoda

Handwork Resources

The Best Paper Plane You'll Ever Fly by Klutz Press

Cat's Cradle: A Book of String Figures by Anne Akers Johnson

Feltcraft: Making Dolls, Gifts and Toys by Petra Berger

Kids Knitting: Projects for Kids of All Ages by Melanie Falick

Kids' Paper Airplane Book by Ken Blackburn

Kinder Dolls: A Waldorf Doll-Making Handbook by Maricristin Sealey

The Klutz Book of Knots by John Cassidy

Magic Wool: Creative Activities with Natural Sheep's Wool by Dagmar Schmidt & Freya Jaffke

The Red Wolf by Margaret Shannon

String Games by Richard Darsie

Woodworking for Kids: 40 Fabulous, Fun & Useful Things for Kids to Make by Kevin McGuire

Using Toys the Wrong Way

Allowing toys to be used in ways they were not intended is a wonderful way to build creativity!

puzzle, "Squzzle" or Scramble Squares®, and Varialand wooden puzzle for very young children. Use your own artwork to make an especially unique puzzle by cutting it into pieces the size and shape of your choice. Provide opportunities for children to work puzzles that are too difficult with an older puzzler modeling the process, but also allow simpler puzzles to be put together repeatedly in order to build connections for how things go together.

Brainteasers

Brainteasers are also a wonderful way to get children to begin thinking in different ways. They introduce children to many discovery and scientific inquiry techniques. Start your young children on brainteasing quests by playing "What animal am I?" and "What number am I?" games and other riddles. Play the hot and cold game where you hide an item and the child uses your verbal clues to find it. Move on to scavenger hunts. Provide simple clues leading to hidden objects around the house.

Word games

Play the more traditional games like Scrabble and Password, or make up your own word games together. Try word card games like Quiddler for some more word fun. See Chapter 18, *Words My Way*, for other word association and game ideas.

Strategy Games

Having to think and plan ahead is a skill that is easily practiced using traditional board games. Even very young children enjoy playing strategy games. Chess, checkers, Quoridor™, and Labyrinth™ are among the best to introduce strategy playing to young children. Other games requiring the use of strategy for young children are Uno, Skip-Bo, Dominos, Connect Four, and the regular and Junior versions of the games Apples to Apples and ThinkFun's many games like River Cross and Rush Hour.

FAVORITE FRIENDS AND FIGURES

Some of a child's most creative moments, such as role playing and storytelling, happen in the private moments he has with special stuffed animals, dolls, or other figurines such as Playmobil™ people, plasticine animals, or even an imaginary friend. Take this imaginative play with these special friends further by providing kids adequate alone time with them. Offer opportunities to personify their friends further by making a bed, a swing, or setting up a tea party for Mr. and Mrs. Bear and family.

TRAINS AND TRAIN TABLES

Wooden and plastic trains are all the rage. They've been gracing the floors of many households for decades. Their growing popularity has meant the introduction of the train table, available in various styles and colors. Some, like the one we own, even have convenient drawers to organize all of the trains. While we enjoy the work surface and the extra storage space, they are not practical for creativity's sake. With a train table, the child is confined to one relatively small space to create within. Provide your children opportunities to start thinking beyond the train table. Challenge them in getting the train track to travel off the table, and then when that wears off, be okay with building train routes on the floor where the problem solving can happen to the nth degree.

Play is thought to be the best way intelligence and human potential can unfold. Provide children with tools of the trade. It will give them joy and freedom to create as they refine and develop understanding of their world, imagination, and potential.

Resources for Catalogues that Carry Toys which Nurture Creativity

HearthSong 1-800-325-2502 www.hearthsong.com

Lakeshore Learning Materials 1-800-421-5354 www.lakeshorelearning.com

Magic Cabin www.magiccabin.com

Mindware 1-800-274-6123 www.mindwareonline.com

chapter 8

WONder WorLd

Taking Creativity Outdoors

In 1845, Henry David Thoreau embarked on a two-year experiment when he moved to a second-growth forest around the shores of Walden Pond and lived in a cabin that he built on his friend Ralph Waldo Emerson's land. The experience was immortalized in his book *Walden: Or Life in the Woods* in which he wrote: "Only that day dawns to which we are awake."

On the path to awaken a child's creativity, we sometimes only need to step outdoors. Active outdoor play helps children develop many skills: physical, emotional, social, and cognitive. In addition, it develops their senses of smell, touch, and taste, and the sense of motion through space in ways indoor activities cannot. When children have access to the outdoors, they gain the ability to navigate and an understanding for environments. Even without ready access to special places such as the beach, forests, fields, and streams, we can still find ways to keep connected to the outdoors. Inherent in outdoor experiences is the foundation being set for an exploratory, courageous spirit that will lead children through a lifetime of awakening.

Even the most seasoned fun-seeking families sometimes need ideas to take the outdoor experiences in general beyond our normal functional and exploratory play. Begin with your physical environment: assess your outdoor spaces. Nothing can compare to a run in an open field or play in a mysterious forest, but even a small balcony can be a wonderful outdoor play space. Natural outdoor play spaces stimulate the imagination and engage a sense of curiosity in a way indoor spaces cannot. Help your spaces along by making them safe and child-sized. Provide opportunities for your children to self select the materials they will play with so they can build upon their natural sense of exploration. Towards this end, consider setting up special outdoor areas that stimulate creative play.

STORY CORNER

Setting up a story place is a great place to start. Take your stories outside for the summer. Designate a special corner of your yard, spread a blanket and stock it with a basket of books. Perhaps create it under (or in) a special tree or corner of the garden that lends itself to a quiet break from afternoon play or a noontime story.

OUTDOOR WRITING

Don't get caught thinking that writing needs to occur inside at a designated table or desk. Bring your writing notebooks outside and on nature hikes. Experiment with writing from different perspectives in your yard or in a park. Encourage your children to draw pictures or write poems. Write stories or poems together inspired by the sounds you hear or the squirrel that just stole your apple. Share your stories and pictures. See Chapter 20, *Words My Way,* for more ideas on creative writing.

MUD AND WATER

There's nothing like a mud hole to bring out the creativity in your children and really connect with their senses and the wonders of nature.

Of course sprinklers, pools, and ponds are always a big hit, but try adding simple plastic pipe to the fun for added creativity and problem solving. Provide an array of shapes and configurations with which your child can make waterways. Because they easily snap and unsnap, there is a different configuration each time and it makes for easy cleanup.

See Chapter 12, *Squish! Splat! Smoosh!*, for further exploration into mud holes.

BUILDING OPPORTUNITIES

As children explore the outdoors, many opportunities exist for them to construct. Build birdhouses, unique places to hide in, or use natural materials to make homes for the wood sprites, gnomes, and fairies that may visit in the hours of dawn and dusk. Try whittling and notching a found branch to make a walking stick and unique measuring stick. Add feathers or other decorations to make it extra special. Provide many opportunities and building supplies for children to use their imagination outdoors. See Chapter 3, *Breaking Ground*, for building supply ideas.

BEYOND THE SANDBOX

How can you make your sand or dirt box more than just a place for digging? Try adding rope, pulleys, and buckets. These can be used to lift dirt up and out or across to another part of the yard or even a neighboring balcony. Pulleys can be connected to decks, overhangs, trees... the sky's the limit! Test out different ideas about what it takes to lift heavy loads. Sort, categorize, and graph what you find in different bucketfuls. Explore the wonders of the pulley—what an amazing simple machine!

But don't sit by and let dirt just be dirt! Head over to your sandbox for a paleontological dig—turn ordinary rocks into fossilized bones! Equip your team with the tools of the trade. Keep a bucket by the door complete with paint brushes of different sizes, wooden chisels (often found in clay tool sets), wooden hammers, small metal shovels, and, if you really want to get fancy, a water bottle, a yogurt container, and some Plaster of Paris for wrapping the bones to return to the lab (plastic wrap will also do the job). Then, head out to the dig site (which can be any pile of sand, dirt, etc.). Encourage your junior paleontologist to examine the site carefully and take her time as she uncovers the precious fossils. Brush them

How to Climb a Tree

It is has been said that those who dwell in the beauty of the trees will never grow weary to the mysteries of life.

In the I Can Read Book *Little Bear's Friend* by Else Homelund Minarik, the story begins with Little Bear climbing a tree. During Little Bear's journey to the top of that tree, he encounters a few challenges, a little bit of fear, unsurpassable views, perspective, confidence, and eventually, as the title suggests, a new friend.

Many adults hold onto a memory about climbing trees, either with childhood friends or on solo retreats into the sky to look down on the world. Many children today are not getting this valuable motor skill and confidence building opportunity. A recent study conducted in Sweden showed that young people who not only played outside, but played in natural settings (not just outdoors on play equipment) played more creatively.

Climbing trees offers many opportunities for children to not just develop physically, but also mentally. With every step, children who climb are playing a game of vertical chess, if you will, that has them strategizing, developing mental agility as they make spilt second decisions, and learning psychological balance.

As you begin your tree climbing adventures, keep the following in mind.

Find the Right Tree

The right climbing tree is certainly a treasure when you find it. The perfect climbing tree for a young child is one they can get up into all by themselves, without a parental boost. It would likely have many wide natural Y's that branch out from a short base. It will also be free of tree damaging pests or other signs of decay. For people under four feet, this can be a real challenge, and may mean that you are only playing around the base of a large tree or on fallen trees for a while to get a feel for the experience of playing in natural settings.

Once you do find the right tree, keep coming back to it. Every time you climb it, know that you will be developing the independence and confidence to climb to the top of any challenge. Then, as you grow and when you are ready, move on and find a new favorite tree.

Step by Step

Trees, like people and all that we encounter in life, are living, growing, organic experiences that provide many opportunities for trial and error. Can this branch hold my weight? Can I take that step without slipping? Are those branches close enough for me to step from one to the next?

The perfect climbing tree might have its own knobby pieces spaced naturally apart, but if yours does not, consider using a strong rope to assist your climb or nailing in pieces of wood to make a modified stepladder. A nail into the bark of a mature tree is not thought to be fatally damaging. However, a larger structure such as a hammock, tree house or garden art can put too much stress on the tree that can leave it vulnerable.

Professional tree climbers say that excessive climbing could damage a tree, but they also admit that climbing provides an opportunity to develop appreciation for nature, and that far outweighs any potential damage.

Gain Perspective

Whether or not you have reached the top of the tree you are climbing, take some time to look out on the world from a new perspective. With a view from the treetops, take a deep breath of all that freshness that being up off the ground can give you. Take in the view as a whole, or bring along a collapsible telescope or binoculars to see the views beyond.

Being up in a tree can provide children a respite from daily hustle and bustle, so if it works for you, consider allowing your child to just hang out in the tree. As they grow, that might be the place they go to enjoy a friend, read a book, or just plain rejuvenate themselves.

Fly Down

"I'll fly down," says Little Bear as he plans his exit from the tree. Well, anyone who has ever shimmied up to the top of what seems like the perfect climbing tree, and then turned around to come down, realizes the going up can be the easy part. As a parent, the hardest part can be the witnessing. Support children verbally as they begin their descent. Coach them in facing the tree and stepping down as if coming down a ladder, using some of the same foot and handholds they found along the way. Provide encouragement that communicates your confidence in them as they learn to solve a new kind of problem. At some point, they are ready to make that final leap onto the ground, and you may just see the wings sprout.

So go on, climb a tree. Experience the joy of reaching new heights and hold onto the mysteries that a life among the trees can offer.

off and wrap them for transport. When you're back in the lab, clean and identify them. Save them in a box with labels. Make a map of the dig site for future investigations. Write notes in your journal about your discoveries. Sketch the creature that the bones might have made. Be sure to include those you didn't find (perhaps in a different color).

GARDENING

The wonders of the garden await your family when you explore all it has to offer: finding a plot, planning what to plant, collecting seeds, preparing the soil, exploring helpful critters, daily watering, watching growth, and harvesting. Provide your children with their own gardening tools: gloves, watering can, a child-sized rake, shovel, hoe, and perhaps even their own wheelbarrow.

And don't underestimate the snails. We may consider them pests as they arrive in the early morning hours to nibble on our beans, but kids find them fascinating. If only for a day, delight in the wonders of "Snail Olympics" as you observe them walking a *tight rope* or *racing* over little cups or other obstacles. Experiment with a little squirt of water and see what a bit (or a lot, depending on your perspective) of slime can do!

Many good resources (listed at the end of this chapter) exist for gardening with children. Take advantage of them.

OUTDOOR INTERACTIONS

Create opportunities for interaction with others, the others who dwell outdoors naturally. Make birdhouses or add seeds to a special stump or other low spot to encourage the squirrels. Try learning the calls of ducks, owls, blackbirds, or other birds in your area. Keep track of all the different birds you see and what time of year they come around. Find a special, quiet spot and just take a seat. It's amazing what you can observe and the array of critters that emerge when the world appears to be free of walking feet and talking mouths.

Interactions outdoors need not be limited to the critters; get the neighbors involved too. Set up a place for a puppet show or an outdoor stage. Don't forget the all important lemonade stand or, as Elisabeth Harrod suggests, the ice cream truck!

"Step back in time to the simple pleasures of a hot summer afternoon. You and your learner can have a great time, learn a lot, and make all your friends and neighbors very happy by creating your very own neighborhood ice cream truck. Load up a wagon, wheel barrel, cart, or ice chest on wheels with yummy treats. Include ice cream, frozen banana slices dipped in chocolate, popsicles made from different fruit juices frozen into an ice tray or other small shape with a stick, and fruit smoothies. Don't forgot a cooler, ice, a sign with your options and prices, a box for collecting money that includes change, a towel, cups, bowls, cones, spoons, napkins, and other necessities. The icing on the cake, so to speak, is offering music as you travel through the neighborhood, letting everyone know the ice cream truck is in business! This is a great way to get your child involved in planning, organizing, cooking, shopping, gaining social confidence, using money, writing and drawing, music making, and so many other fun and practical skills. Think of all the happy neighbors and extra income you'll have!"

STREWING

Strewing is the very fine art of placing items in seemingly random locations. It provides the opportunity for creativity by allowing a child to stumble upon materials in a natural way, thereby encouraging their exploration, without the child feeling pressured. Throughout the year, place interesting items in high traffic areas for your children to discover without you ever saying a word. Watch as their creativity unfolds.

Rotate items (in prominent, easily stumbled upon places) such as seed packets, buckets, shovels, magnifying glasses, muffin tins, binoculars, chopsticks, bird books, plastic crates, harvested corn, and all the other materials that would be required for any of the above mentioned ideas. A little bit of outdoor strewing can go a long way!

CHANGING WEATHER

As summer turns to fall, many children delight in the wonders of leaves floating to the ground. If you are lucky enough to live in such an area, help your children to rake the leaves into a lawn maze. Run, walk backwards, or take your toy trucks or tricycle through it.

Raindrop Fun

Just like the two little children in Dr. Seuss' book *The Cat in the Hat*, on rainy days children often feel the need to stay inside. Regardless of the weather, there are many opportunities for creative adventures. Rainy days are no exception. Collect rain as it falls, either in a jar doubling as a rain gauge or on a piece of watercolor paper sprinkled with a bit of powdered tempera paint. Take time to discover the wonders of the rain as it gathers in puddles. Float things in it. Measure its depth.

A Snow Ball

And when the raindrops freeze and turn to snow, the possibilities seem even more unlimited. Make snow huts, complete with trails leading up to them and all the supplies your snow people need. Practice your sculpture skills and think outside the snowman. Pretend to be a snowflake and dance through the yard. Float down and melt as you touch the sidewalk.

Windy Days

Whatever you do, don't ignore the wind; it offers great opportunity for exploration. Make windsocks or flags to measure the wind's strength. Try your hand at making a windmill or wind chimes out of tiny bells or shells and string. Experiment with how the wind helps things move. Attach a small figurine to a plastic bag or light cloth (such as a playsilk) to make a parachute and see what the wind does with it. Don't forget to experiment with flying a kite. Can you make it flip or dive?

Afterhours

Star-gazing and observing the ever-changing sky are also wonderful ways to extend the hours of outdoor play. On evening walks, draw pictures and tell stories about the moon as it transitions through its phases throughout the month. Search for constellations. Watch the space station during its most visible times, which can sometimes be very early dawn or at dusk, depending on the time of year.

As you step outdoors and experience the wonders of your own creativity meet the wonders of the natural world, feel the awakening happen. Creativity, imagination, and thinking outside the sandbox will surely dawn.

Picture Books about Outdoor Fun

All I See is Part of Me by Chara M. Curtis

Cloudy With a Chance of Meatballs by Judi Barrett

Earthdance by Joanne Ryder

Fairy Houses by Tracy L. Kane

Fairy Boats by Tracy L. Kane

Have You Seen Trees? by Joanne Oppenheim

Hello Grand Mamoon! by Donna Steinmann

Henry Hikes to Fitchburg by D. B. Johnson

Henry Builds a House by D. B. Johnson

In My New Yellow Shirt by Eileen Spinelli

The Listening Walk by Paul Showers

Mud by Mary Lynn Ray

Mud Puddle by Robert N. Munsch

Miss Rumphius by Barbara Cooney

Red Rubber Boot Day by Mary Lyn Ray

The Snail's Spell by Joanne Ryder

The Snowy Day by Ezra Jack Keats

Twilight Comes Twice by Ralph Fletcher

Weslandia by Paul Fleischman

When the Root Children Wake Up by Audrey Wood

When the Wind Stops by Charlotte Zolotow

Wild Child by Lynn Plourde

Winter's Tale: An Original Pop-Up Journey by Robert Sabuda

Resources for Outdoor Play

Everybody Loves Ice Cream: The Whole Scoop on America's Favorite Treat by Shannon Jackson Arnold

The Kids' Book of Weather Forecasting: Build a Weather Station, Read the Sky & Make Predictions! by Meteorologists Mark Breen & Kathleen Friestad

Kids Garden: The Anytime, Anyplace Guide to Sowing & Growing Fun by Avery Hart & Paul Mantell

The Kids' Nature Book - 365 Indoor/Outdoor Activities and Experiences by Warner Shedd

Kids' Wildlife Book: Exploring Animal Worlds Through Indoor/Outdoor Experiences by Susan Milord

Rainy Day Play by Nancy Fusco Castaldo

Roots, Shoots, Buckets and Boots by Sharon Lovejoy

Summer Fun: 60 Activities for a Kid-Perfect Summer by Susan Williamson

Sunflower Houses by Sharon Lovejoy

chapter 9

to pirate ships and castle moats

Creating Costuming Experiences that Take You Places

"How now spirit! Wither wander you?"

No, this is not Master Puck, Merry Wanderer of the Night, but rather an enthusiastic four year-old running gallantly through the house and stopping suddenly at a stuffed giraffe so thoughtfully placed on the roadside.

Aah . . . the costumes, and their inevitable effect on creative expression, are at it again.

Human beings have had a long tradition and desire for dressing up as a means of creative expression. From tribal traditions to early religious celebrations to the masquerade ball, the art of costuming has prevailed. Perhaps this art is beyond our control and part of a deeper psychological and physical need.

Circling villages in costumes and masks are ancient African traditions believed to bring good fortune and healing to the village. Today we see this represented in Carnivale celebrations through the Caribbean and South America. Traditionally in Africa, natural objects such as bones, grasses, feathers, shells, and even hooves were used as props or symbols of something greater.

Mirrors in the Dress up Corner

For the obvious reason of allowing children to see how they have changed when donning a costume, mirrors are often placed in the dress up corner, or near to costume supplies. The use of mirrors has been touted for children to learn about themselves, their bodies, and knowing where they are. When children are very young (as young as six months) they are interested in mirror images. As they grow older (especially young girls entering school age), they become increasingly interested in mirrors for different reasons. Be conscious of this when setting up dress up areas. If you feel it is important to have a mirror in your dress up area, place it in a more discreet location so the focus is more on the dressing up than the checking up.

Feathers were often used as a symbol of rising above, traveling to other worlds, and growing into a more spiritual being, one connected to his or her creative center.

Donning costumes and masks has also been traditional in religious celebrations throughout the centuries. For thousands of years in Hindu cultures, people have been dressing up and reenacting the return of Ganesha, portraying an excited Hanuman, creating depictions of the Ramayana, and recreating a flute playing Shiva. In Jewish customs recreations of the Scroll of Esther have been portrayed during the Purim holiday. The masquerade ball, to celebrate dynastic events, marriages, and just for sheer fun, originated in the late-Medieval court.

The spirit of masquerading, and its promise of escapism, decadence, and fantasy, is truly timeless. From the youngest members of the society to the eldest players, costumes have likewise remained ageless. Wearing costumes, masks, or just simple props, was historically and still remains a wonderful way to build and enhance creativity.

When children dress up, they are provided a unique opportunity to express originality. They can pair things that conventionally don't go together, explore possibilities and create alternate realities. They can play with ideas and see how they might work themselves out in different ways.

Costuming adds a unique way to role play situations and allows children to solve problems in many ways. What would a knight do in just such a situation? In the same way, dressing up allows children to make connections to their world, explore what they might be reading or learning about, and develop deeper understanding.

In a world where schedules and to-do lists often dictate their lives, children don't always have great control over their environment. Dressing up, costume boxes, and dramatic play all provide children the opportunity to add to and change the environment in their own ways.

Key to the building of creative thinking is that we develop curiosity about specific things and a curious nature in general. Dramatization offers children yet another way to develop an experimental attitude. Children can respond to stimuli in unique ways and test and evaluate skills they are learning.

Developing autonomy and self-reliance is a key component of living a creative life. When children take part in a costuming experience and express their own ideas through drama, they are practicing that independence.

Increasingly, Halloween events across the nation in which students from elementary schools parade around in their costumes, are being cancelled. In October 2005, one school district spokeswoman from Washington said, "It takes time and when kids dress up in costumes it's a distraction. It takes away from learning." Sadly, costume parades, parties, and exploration time (whether related to Halloween or not) are cancelled in schools and communities around the country for much the same reason.

Will costuming and dramatic play be a distraction and take away from learning? No! It will add to it tenfold! In fact, dressing up is an outlet and enhances and stimulates creativity for all ages. Through dress up play, children can learn new skills, imaginatively role play ideas and life skills, and play together cooperatively.

Most important to keep in mind when allowing opportunities for students to experiment with costumes is to respect the process. It is sometimes difficult to observe a child's creative play

What Do I Put in a Costume Box?

Purchasing costumes and accessories is certainly an option, but before you run out to the costume store, check around your own home for dress-up treasures. Start with a few basic supplies you might have already and add to it over time.

Ideas for the Costume Box:

- scarves and ties
- bandanas
- textured or colored pieces of cloth (burlap, silk, velvet, wool, etc.)
- old baby blankets
- lab coats
- Grandma's old shoes
- aprons
- hats (sailor, construction, farmer, cowboy, engineer, crowns, fancy plumed, etc.)
- ears and noses for a variety of animals
- costume jewelry
- glasses and goggles
- wigs
- tunics
- vests
- ruffled (or otherwise fun) shirts
- fancy dresses and skirts
- purses and bags
- gloves
- masks
- wings
- bits and pieces of Halloween costumes

and not control the direction it takes. One teacher described it as the *duct tape method*. She said, "On those days when you feel like jumping in and taking over, just imagine yourself duct taping your mouth shut. Just allow their creativity to emerge."

To respect the process also means providing access. Provide a spot in the home where costumes and props are held even if they are not always used. In the home, costumes can be stored in a variety of ways: a large basket, an old trunk, a cardboard box, a corner in the playroom or your child's room, a designated closet where you keep your dress-up supplies and/or pegs on the wall. A hat rack, hooks, or hanging clips keep the costumes in sight and in mind. For more discreet storage of costume items to be brought out during special choice times, keep them in a trunk, a basket, a suitcase, or even a closet. If you use a closet to store items, make sure it is one that is accessible to children when the dramatic urge hits. While it is important to have a storage spot for dress up supplies, keeping a few items out, such as capes or other special pieces, makes them easily accessible and will encourage dress up time. So remember the saying "out of sight, out of mind" when you are creating your dress up space.

Once you have made a commitment to allow your children to have access to costume supplies, and perhaps compiled and arranged them in a special corner of your room, what next? As children begin to know what they have available to them and have increased opportunities to use those props in different ways, they will become more creative in their uses. Towards that end, consider setting up a stage, a place for dramatic play to be acted out and culminate. If you have space for it, use cinder blocks and a sheet of plywood covered with a strip of carpeting to make a stand-alone stage. Add some curtains on a wire to set the stage apart from other spaces in the room.

Your own home is the best place to find items to fill a costume box! When cleaning out your closets and attics, look for outdated or worn-out things you no longer use. It's amazing what you'll find. After-Halloween sales are the best places to find fun and unique items to put in costume boxes. On the day after Halloween, we've managed to procure never before worn lion and dinosaur costumes as well as some wonderful face paints, all for less than two dollars on Ebay. Second hand shops usually pull out

Pictures Books About Dressing Up

Dress-Up by Marcia Leonard

The Hat by Jan Brett

Max's Dragon Shirt by Rosemary Wells

Shoes from Grandpa by Mem Fox

The Rainy Day Grump by Deborah Eaton

What Can I Be? By Cari Meister

What Can You Do With a Shoe? By Beatrice Schenk De
    Regniers

all of their costumes and costume supplies during the month of October. Head in on November first and you are likely to find some real deals. Watch garage sale ads for old costumes and costume supplies. Often, many a Renaissance Faire and old theatre stashes are liquidated through the seamstress' personal garage sale. You'll also likely find wonderful accessory pieces hiding out in garage sales or flea markets.

So dust off those old treasures lurking in Grandma's attic. Always be on the look out for that little bit of material or shiny headdress and wing set that will turn any rainy day into a *Midsummer Night's Dream*. Know those moments of creativity and imaginative roleplay will continue to build thoughtful learners in your home. Happy Pretending!

chapter 10

HoLd My HaNd

Cooperative Play and Games
as an Opportunity for Creativity

"I feel sad when someone has to lose."
—Maya, 4 years-old

We live in a large running community with a major university that has much invested into their track and field program, so much so that there is also a junior track club for children ages 3-12. Both my husband and I were runners at one point and found joy in it. When our son turned three years-old we thought it would be fun to go see the track and have some fun running. Categorized by age in appropriately sized heats, all the children lined up for the 100 yard dash. The whistle blew. Dazed and confused by the fervor of their parents, the three year-olds toddled down the track. We watched to see how our son would react. He'd never been in this type of competitive situation before. He turned to the child next to him and reached out for his hand. Together, they trotted slowly down the track, gleefully gathering new hand holders along the way.

The very next week, I read an account of a Peace Corps volunteer who had attempted to set up a foot race with a group of children in a small village in Africa. When she gave the signal to start running, all the children joined hands and ran the length of the race together. The idea of competition was foreign to them. The culture of cooperation was clearly evident.

Such has been the nature of games for as long as we can trace their origins. Throughout the histories of Asia, Africa, and the Americas, games have existed in cooperative form and continue to be so. Children from cultures around the world are found making their own toys, playing hand games, and making music . . . together. With the introduction of the Olympic Games in Ancient Greece, games moved from purely cooperative play to exclusive competitive play among and for men.

In the United States, we focus on the competitive factor of games. Competition is such a part of our lives. We compete in the business world, academics, and even socially as we strive to be the one on the block with the most *toys*. As parents, by modeling and reinforcing this need to compete, we pass it on to children early, either explicitly or unconsciously.

However, in the Sensori-Motor stage of development (up to age two), children are unable to grasp the concept of rules for games. It is not until the Concrete Operational Stage (ages seven or eight) that children develop a true understanding of the significance of rules and abstract structures. Therefore, creative play and cooperation are natural instincts for very young children. When parents provide these opportunities to disconnect from other human beings by playing games that have a winner, the instincts become more distant. Once you designate one winner, what does that make everyone else?

Some would argue that taking on the role of *loser* is a fact of life and a lesson that should be taught early and often. That would be true if our goal was disconnection from each other. Interestingly enough, that is exactly what we are teaching children when we set up ways for children to practice competition and designate winners and losers in play.

As children play together cooperatively, they practice the important skill of working together towards a common goal. Creatively speaking, the ability to solve problems and think about ideas and solutions is a cooperative venture. With more minds contributing to the process, varied solutions are more likely to happen. New ideas for play or classic games which have been innovated upon offer a wonderful outlet for creativity and building thinking. The result: children learn how to share, take turns, and ultimately, to respect the ideas and input of others.

THE FAMILY THAT PLAYS TOGETHER

The best way to teach children any skill is to model the behavior. The more adults engage in play with children the more children will learn about the world around them.

As children construct play together with multiple participants, they are gaining practice in being creative.

Usually when adults engage in play, for developmental reasons and due to the fact that they have internalized the competitive nature, they are more bound by rules than the children. Allow yourself the same freedom your child feels and let the game take its own direction. Recognize that if your child wants to move the pieces on the Candy Land board in all different directions, it can be creative exploration, not cheating.

While you play the game, let children make up their own rules as ideas come to them. Negotiate what will and will not be allowed. Just decide on it together. As children grow, they will have gained an entire repertoire of games they have innovated and ways of playing. Furthermore, they will take this skill of innovation into other areas of their lives as they grow.

The End of the Game

Children often don't want the game to end. Having to deal with someone being a loser is compounded with the fact that the game is over. A game that is truly fun to play does not need to abruptly end just because one person has put down all their cards, made it to a certain place on the game board, or scored a certain amount of points. Continue playing until the players are emotionally done. Give time limits instead of point limits. Begin the game with a timer if necessary. If you, as the adult, become bored with the game, try not to end it abruptly. Instead, give your child a warning about the timeline of the game and what will happen next. "I'm feeling almost done playing. Let's play for three more minutes and then read a book." Or offer the opportunity to return to the game at a later time or date. Coming back to a game later that evening or another day creates schema for children and reinforces the idea of ongoing projects, which are valuable for creativity to fully blossom. Most of all, play for the fun of playing.

THE GAMES WE PLAY

As we assess the important aspects of play with which we want children to grow, games we play start to take on a different meaning. If the overarching message is that we want to nurture an empathic attitude, encourage working together, and value other people's contributions, then we must analyze, and perhaps alter, the games we play.

Parachute Play

Parachutes are often made of bright multi-colored nylon with reinforced handles. They are great fun for both children and adults to play with and can be purchased from athletic supply stores or early childhood suppliers. You can use a large sheet to simulate the real thing. Playsilks, light and airy colored pieces of silk usually measuring 3 x 9 feet, are also a wonderful opportunity for even just two children to activate parachute type play.

The opportunity for innovation is ever present in the parachute. Make small and large waves together. Sit and make a see saw motion. Roll balls along the top of the parachute and work together to keep the balls from bouncing off or try to get all the balls to roll into the center of the parachute. Create a cave by lifting the parachute high into the air. To work, all of these games require working together towards a common goal.

Sand Play

Sandbox play offers a super avenue for kids to work together to build roadways, dig tunnels, transport dirt and rocks, or create a bakery. While some parents are leery of bringing toys to public parks and sandboxes for fear of conflict ensuing, the continued practice in sharing and creating together is certainly beneficial.

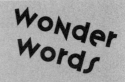

"If smiles are any indication of joy, you will quickly observe that highly organized competitive sport is not for joy."
—Terry Orlick
The Cooperative Sports and Games Book

Balls

Playing with balls does not need to result in hurt bodies or hurt feelings. It is enough for kids to pass the ball back and forth, pretend the ball is something else, or send the ball down hills to each other. Set up outdoor bowling games or make obstacle courses to dribble or pass through.

For young children, it is more about experimenting with the nature of what a ball can do than who can make it into the goal. Consider investing in a large canvas ball (sometimes called Earth balls) or a body ball for children to play with, roll along their bodies, or work together to keep up in the air. In the same way, for very young children or for children who are intimidated by fast paced ball play, use balloons to initiate interesting and innovative play.

Play in the Absence of Toys or Games

Some of the most creative moments happen with the absence of toys or other props, when children have only their bodies and their imaginations. Start them thinking about making a human obstacle course, creating a snake, becoming other animals, making a spiral, rowing their boat across the playground, making tunnels, or laying down to make an interesting shape. In the absence of toys or games, children's play often reaches new heights: they often pretend to go on journeys to far off or made up lands.

Party Games

When we gather children together we often desire an organized game for children to play. *New York Times* reporter Nicholas Kristof accounts trying to teach a group of Japanese children to play musical chairs, who kept politely moving to let others sit. Certainly, our need to be competitive is a cultural aspect. Because

Cooperative Game Books

Cooperative Games and Activities by Sambhava and Josette Luvmour

The Cooperative Sports and Games Book: Challenge Without Competition by Terry Orlick

Every Kid Can Win by Terry Orlick

Everyone Wins! The Second Cooperative Sports and Games Book by Terry Orlick

For the Fun of It by Marta Harrison

Games Enjoyed By Children Around the World Edited by Mary Esther McWhirter

Games of the World: How to Make Them, How to Play Them, How They Came to Be by Swiss Committee for UNICEF

Games We Should Play in School by Frank Aycox

Hopscotch, Hangman, Hot Potatoes and Ha, Ha, Ha by Jack Maguire

The Little Hands Playtime Book: 50 Activities to Encourage Cooperation & Sharing by Regina Curtis

More New Games and Playful Ideas from the New Games Foundation by Andrew Flugelman

The New Games Book by Andrew Flugelman

New Games for the Whole Family by Dale LeFevre

Non-Competitive Games for People of All Ages by Susan Butler

Winning Through Cooperation by Terry Orlick

parties are also cultural, that competitive spirit emerges in the games we play at children's parties. Consider offering alternatives where there are many kings on the mountain, and ultimately where everybody wins.

Board Games

We've entered a new millennium of games. Aisles and aisles of board games exist for children. It can be a difficult task to choose a game that will be both fun and creative for children and adults. Few board games offer varied options for how they will be played. Most games designate a winner: the person who makes it around the board first, who captures all the pieces, or who collects the most money. Some would call this a reflection of real life in the twenty-first century.

Mahatma Gandhi said, "Be the change you wish to see in the world." If we strive towards a world where children grow into creative and thinking adults who have the skills to solve unique problems, we must allow our children to innovate on the games they are given and offer them the control.

Certain games we play are surely competitive in nature. Strategy games, such as chess, while being wonderful thinking games, are based on the premise that we are separate from each other, usually divided by borders. Camps are set up and the goal is to destroy the leader. In the case of chess, capture or kill the king. Many children are either devastated or overjoyed by this idea. Without needing to ban these types of games, because they do offer children many wonderful thinking and planning opportunities, we can consider optional ways to play them from time to time. Recognize how simple modifications can make the experience a team effort and deepen our personal connections.

Create Your Own Games

The more practice children get in using materials available to them in unique ways, the more they will be able to think outside the box. Present them with options to make up string games. Make mazes out of recycled materials. Make large-scale board games that require human pieces moving through the game.

See Chapter 7, *Wonder Tools*, for more ideas about handcraft and making toys.

Solving Problems Together

Make solving problems a game. Encourage team effort at home by sharing responsibilities with your children. Have at least one "chore" or activity designated as a family job. Work in the garden together. Pick up toys together. Instead of competing for who can pick up the toys fastest, set a timer and see if you can beat the clock, not each other.

Role Playing

When children engage in role playing activities, they are truly able to get to the heart of their feelings about situations and spend some time in someone else's shoes.

Provide opportunities for simulation play (see Chapter 7, *Wonder Tools*) so children can gain experience in acting out scenarios and discovering solutions for them.

Games are wonderful. As we bring a more mindful attitude towards what, why, and how we play them, we find a multitude of opportunities for joining hands and running together towards creative growth.

chapter 11

give me space

Quiet Places and Special Spots that Nurture Creativity

"In a minute, Mommy. I'm busy," Aidan said while closing the door of the cave, one of this four year-old's most treasured spots. Bear and Zippy the Lion huddle close to the flashlight as Aidan tells stories. "Would you like more tea?" his mom overhears from just outside the entrance.

Like all human beings, children need private spaces and time alone to uncover their individual and unique identities. On top of a six-hour school day, many children are involved in soccer, ballet, piano lessons, and scouts. While all of these activities can add dimension and enrich their lives, children need time away from their hectic schedules in order to tap into their creativity and fully develop their sense of self. Encouraging our children to have some alone time and some settling time provides an opportunity for them to blossom.

Away from the everyday barrage of activities and people, children are able to have the space that allows their creativity to emerge. If we can create some quiet times in their lives, we encourage children to think more, think differently, and to solve problems.

Even if you are thinking your child does not like to be "alone" or if living arrangements are tight, the possibilities for creative special places and spots are wide-ranging.

HAPPY, HOMEY HOUSES

Play houses can be made very inexpensively and out of a variety of materials. You can use existing structures or start from scratch. Convert an old dog house or greenhouse into a play house, or make one out of an old refrigerator box which you can usually get for free from your local appliance store.

If you don't already have a structure in place, you have many options to choose from. Consider using plastic HDEP piping, available at any hardware or home improvement store, to create a unique frame; it is a fabulous (and inexpensive) material that you can use to create wall, window, and door openings easily. Piping is also great because you can change the configurations as your child grows or changes interests. What was once a play house can become a rocket, store, lemonade stand, or library in a matter of minutes.

House building is a great opportunity to get creative with your kids and the materials you choose. Little touches can completely change your locale. Use bubble wrap to line the outside of your structure and call it "Hailey's Ice House." Hang mirrors on the walls to create "Montana's Fun House." Use corrugated cardboard to create "Ian's O.K. Corral." Playsilks are also wonderful building materials that can become whatever a child can imagine.

LOFT LIVIN'

Lofts are great utilizers of space, raised structures taking advantage of the room between the ceiling and floor. They are the quintessential example of a special place for kids to retreat, to experience respite from daily activity.

Building a loft does not necessarily mean starting from scratch. Consider what Elisabeth and Jon Harrod did when they wanted to create a special spot for their son, Will. They wanted a place he could always go separate of baby brother. So instead of building a loft from scratch, Jon and Elisabeth converted an empty space that was originally intended as a storage space into a loft. They added a small round window and a homemade ladder. What would have been an ordinary storage closet was turned into Will's museum, private spot, and all around creative space.

Lofts are also among the most permanent of special places. Obviously, it is important for a loft to be a sound structure, so consider a carpenter and check on building codes when you are planning to build your loft. See the end of this chapter for resources related to loft building.

COZY CAVES

Caves are fantastic little nooks that a child finds inside or out, built with pillows or set up under desks or tables. While they can easily and spontaneously be made indoors on a rainy day, one of the most pleasurable places for a cave is outdoors. Find a bush or hedge that could use some trimming and go to work. Carve out a spot and maybe even some tiny cave spots inside to be used for shelving. This is a super activity to do during the days when you are pruning and readying your garden for summer growth and will continue to be a great snow cave come winter.

TENT TIME

Tents can be made from just about anything or you can set up store bought ones. Use old sheets and blankets and clothespins or clips to create cozy spots in tent form. Set them up indoors or out. Erect tents under built-ins (such as desks), atop beds, in obscure corners, and over chairs; they are only limited by your imagination. Leauriy Polk remembers her tent time in urban Michigan summers, under a blanket attached to a chain link fence, as "the very best place to be!"

Use them as a special reading or creative play spot, to take a nap, or just for a respite from a busy day and watch as the creativity unfolds. Tents can be among the best special spaces because they maximize the undersides of chairs and tables and are easy to put away.

Stories About Special Places and Spots

In My Treehouse by Alice Schertle

The Magic Fort by Juanita Havill

The Magic Treehouse Series by Mary Pope Osborne

Oliver Pig and the Best Fort Ever by Jean Van Leeuwen and
   Ann Schweninger

Treehouse Tales by Anne Isaacs

A Quiet Place by Douglas Wood

TERRIFIC TREE HOUSES

Tree houses are certainly magical places, but who says they must
be expensive or difficult to make?

Consider a departure from the trendy popularity of immense
backyard structures built by a company and take on the task as a
family. John Anderson's daughter had been asking her dad to
build a tree house for years. One summer it finally happened.
Together, they planned, prepared, and built the tree house of her
dreams. It wasn't elaborate or flashy, but it was simply perfect for
her. "She spends hours up there!" John now proclaims, "I hear her
making up all kinds of worlds and really using her imagination!
What was I waiting for?"

But wait! A tree house need not even be in the trees. The mind
is powerful enough to make whatever you call a tree house into a
tree house. This special spot can be made out of the top or even
underside of a deck or on balconies. Consider adding a slide or
fireman's pole for easy escapes. Or take your tree house adventures indoors and make one atop a bunk bed or in a playroom.
Painting the walls surrounding your house structure will instantly
take you into the woods.

CREATIVE CLOSETS

Finding a special place in your home can sometimes be a question
of space. Consider opening up a closet to your child's imagination.

Small enough to cozy up to a few favorite stuffed friends, closets can be among the favorite special places that a child can have. If the space is cozy enough, with soft pillows or a small comfy chair, it will invite even the most social child to take a few minutes of private time.

In addition to your child's wealth of imaginative stores, you can help the process along by creating a stage or puppet show area in closets. Use cement blocks, wood cut the size of the closet, and curtains instead of the doors to easily and inexpensively turn your broom closet into a creative space for your child. Decorative lights, a flashlight, or an inexpensive push light would finalize a grand space.

LET'S MAKE A TIPI

Tipis are easy and fun to build and can be made from a variety of materials for use inside or out. Use bamboo poles, plastic pipe, 2x2's, or branches the day after pruning to create the framing structure. Tie the tops together with strong twine. If used outside, you can also slightly bury each pole for added security and to make them slightly more permanent. They can be a small structure that fit just one or two children or made large enough for the entire family's nightly story time. To cover the tipi frame, use bed sheets, quilts, fun fabric, a tarp or even pieces of crumpled paper bag sewn together.

HOLY HUTS!

Making huts together can be a great opportunity for your young ones to learn more about housing around the world. These special spots are along the same order as building tipis, just not necessarily in the same shape as a tipi. Still, you can use the same materials (bamboo or other poles) to ground the structure and then add a roof that is whatever shape you desire. Huts can be created as long houses or round houses by adding long grass or hay to the outside structure or along the rooftop.

A SECRET GARDEN

Never underestimate the power of beans; just ask Jack. Using what you are already planting in your yard to create special spots will not only enhance your child's life, but will probably also get them more involved in gardening. When you are planting your beans, sunflowers, walking stick cabbages, elephant garlic, or anything else that grows tall, try planting it in two rows that can be guided together at the top to create a special place inside. For more ideas on gardening and outdoor play, see Chapter 8, *Wonder World*.

BREATHING ROOMS

With the busy schedules we all keep and the go, go, go rhythm of life as we know it, taking time to slow down and take a breath was probably never more important.

Thich Nhat Hanh, Zen master, poet, scholar, and teacher, suggests families set up "Breathing Rooms," a place where it is safe for any member of the family to be alone, take refuge, smile, reflect, restore themselves, or just breathe. "Every civilized family should have such a room, because in each house there are rooms for everything: a place for eating, a place for watching television, a place for guests, a place to do laundry. We have all kind of rooms, except the kind of room we need the most, a room where we can restore our peace, we can restore our dignity."

Having at least one private space in your home that is separate from family happenings may offer the respite a child needs to feel fully settled. It can provide a place where importance is put on rejuvenating the body, alleviating anxieties, and ultimately looking at mental and physical health with a preventive approach. Other family members may find the space to be just as fulfilling. If space is limited in your home, designate a breathing corner, a special pillow or space just outside the home, perhaps a covered porch or deck.

SCAVENGED SPOTS

If you have yet to discover the treasure of second hand stores, recycling centers, garage sales, or flea markets, you may want to

take a look when you begin to think about setting up special places and spots for your children. Consider tapping into your local Freecycle network (www.freecycle.org), a free online recycling organization in which members offer what they don't use anymore and can make requests for items for which they are searching.

Look to the more unique ways of getting your children to spend a little time alone unleashing their creativity. Think beyond the *normal* use for items you may come across. You might find an old claw foot tub just waiting to be set up in that empty corner of your house. Add some pillows and voila! An instant cozy, creative thinking spot.

ACCENTS AND ACCESSORIES

As mentioned in earlier chapters, helping your children add their own special flare to your everyday life, and modeling it yourself, is a great exercise in creativity. You may wish to include the following items when setting up your special spots:

Lookouts

Create a lookout area in your special places by adding a telescope, binoculars, or periscope if your child wants to pretend he is underwater. Make them from paper towel rolls, piping, rolled newspaper, or buy them already made.

Steering Wheels

Old car and boat steering wheels can add hours of fun to your child's special spot. You can also make your own using old bicycle wheels, cardboard, or an old frisbee.

THE UNDER-THE-KITCHEN-TABLE CAVE

1. Cover a table with an old tablecloth that reaches almost all the way to the ground.

2. Make a doorway by cutting a slit up the side that is halfway from the tabletop.

3. Add windows by cutting holes and replacing tablecloth material with clear plastic.

4. Let the kids decorate the inside or outside of the "cave" with markers or fabric paint.

Communication Systems

A key component to encouraging children taking some alone time to build creativity is that they know you can be reached easily. Children are more likely to spend time alone if you are not far from sight or sound. Offer some simple walkie-talkies to stay in communication. See Chapter 3, *Breaking Ground*, for ideas in finding and setting up communication systems that will work for your family.

Sitting Areas

Take a look around your house to find the perfect furnishings for your child's special spot. Pillows can be among the best of choices for furniture. Being low to the ground makes for a cozy feel. Attach metal rings to the corners of pillows to connect them together to make chairs and small sofas. Consider hammocks and swings to make an especially relaxing sitting place. Stumps also make perfect chairs and tables for your outdoor special places.

Sinks or Basins

Dishwashing, clothes washing, cleaning and peeling imaginary vegetables, or even becoming an aquarium may be uses for your child's own sink. Of course, it needs not have running water, but any washbasin or sink from your local recycling center will be a source of hours of fun and imaginative play. As an inexpensive alternative, provide your child with a simple stainless steel bowl to use as a sink.

Digging Areas

Adding a sand box, or something else that encourages a tactile experience, to your special space is wonderful! Even if your spot is indoors, this can be done. Use plastic tubs with lids or culvert pipes to create a sand area. If sand is a medium you do not wish to delve into, try using small rocks, pebbles, oatmeal, beans, barley, or rice as an alternative. A plywood top cut the size of your opening instantly turns your sand area into a useful table. If you are outside, consider carving out the center of an existing stump and filling it with sand, tiny rocks, or making a mud hole.

Other Possible Additions

Let your child's uniqueness shine through by having her choose items to complete that special spot. You may consider adding the following:

- Signs (closed/open, private, keep out, "Come in!" or "Ian's Place")
- Buzzers or knockers
- Slides, poles, or knotted rope for entry and exit
- Flooring—Use throw rugs, mats, or square rubber floor pieces available from home improvement centers. Even the old linoleum or carpet you just pulled out will do the trick.
- Your child's artwork
- Shelves to keep treasures or books
- Lights or lanterns
- Flags or banners

However you decide to create your child's special places and spots, achieve it together and with love. What will result is a distinctive corner of the world that nurtures creativity, confidence, and pride.

Resources

How to Build Treehouses, Huts and Forts by David Stiles
Fun Projects for You and the Kids by David Stiles
The Treehouse Book by Peter Nelson

Swings, Slides, and Other Accessories:

Childlife
800-467-9464
http://www.childlife.com

Gorilla Play Sets, Inc.
1925 Shiloh Road Building 1
Kennesaw, GA 30144
800-882-0272

Playnix Company
888-PLAYNIX
http://www.playnix.com

Playsilks and Silk Canopies:

Aesop's Room
222 D Street, STE 10
Davis, CA 95616
530-753-0243
http://www.aesopsroom.com

Island Treasure Toys
359 Main Street
Yarmouth, ME 04096
888-794-5388
http://www.islandtreasuretoys.com

Plans for Building Lofts and Loft Beds:

Stiles Designs
4 Albertine Lane
East Hampton, NY 11937
800-444-6483
http://www.stilesdesigns.com

Tipi and Tent Materials:

Authentic Tipis:
Straw Bale Trading Post
P.O. Box 126
Moyie Springs, ID 83845
208-267-1086
http://www.strawbaletradingpost.com/Tipis.html

Children's Tipis:

Grandma's Teepees
2113 El Rancho Circle
Hemet, CA 92545
951-765-6245
http://teepees.com

Hammacher Schlemmer & Company, Inc.
800-321-1484

Teepees for Kids
http://www.teepeesforkids.com

chapter 12

SQUISH! SPLAT! SMOOSH!

Making Messes and Getting Dirty

Gooey-goppy. . . squishy-sloppy. . . smooshy-gooshy. . . magnificiently-splooshy! Oh that indescribable wondrous feeling of a slimy substance slipping through our fingers.

While sometimes reluctantly, we are drawn to that feeling. It intrigues us and ultimately has the potential to make colossal, even unwanted, messes. As a parent living in our results-oriented society, you are likely inundated with messages including all kinds of fancy ideas and tricky ways to get your child to clean up after his or herself, how to prevent messes in the first place, and even including the idea that making a mess is somehow an attempt at defiance or testing of limits. Don't be fooled.

Messes are often a direct by-product of learning. Not that one must always be in the middle of a huge mess to inspire learning, but it is definitely a factor in helping a child to tap into his or her creativity. Messes, and just plain messy substances, offer sensory experiences that provide children with an opportunity to use logic, explore spatial skills, develop fine motor and sensory skills, as well as to encourage knowledge of natural materials and creative exploration. Children need messes. Not just when they are babies and toddlers trying to make sense of their world, but well into their childhood. Messes help them to build on what they already know. "If a child doesn't learn to make a mess, he may not learn to use his mind in an open-ended way," said Dr. Jane Healy, educator and author of *Your Child's Growing Mind*. As we are establishing an environment for children to create and think more, we can provide children with opportunities to learn to use their minds in those unrestricted ways.

LEARN TO MAKE A MESS

As human beings, we have an inherent need to make order out of the world. As discussed in Chapter 3, order and organization are definitely good things. The flip side is simply the ability to let go of order, if only for moments at a time, to take steps towards achieving a higher goal. In this case, thinking outside of the box and developing a more creative self can be achieved by taking risks and exploring new substances.

Some children, particularly those with Sensory Integration Dysfunction, do not appreciate a hand dripping with a foreign gooey substance. If your child has hesitations about sensory exploration, get messy with them, for "a parent's joyful participation may be just what a child needs to dig in," said Healy. For a child who really just cannot, for whatever reason, engage in sensory activities, put a little space between the messy substance and the little fingers by using chopsticks, offering gloves, or putting fingerpaints inside closed plastic bags. Then continue to provide children with ongoing sensory experiences in order to lessen its mysteriousness. Some parents find it helpful to make a physical or mental checklist to make sure their kids get ongoing sensory experiences. Ask yourself: did my child . . . play outdoors? . . . have opportunity to use fingers to paint? . . . mix ingredients, play with dough, or some other tactile experience? . . . feel something interesting or unusual?

CONSTRUCTIVELY MESSY

More and more, children are losing their connection with nature, simply because they are spending more time indoors than ever before. Clean kid syndrome is widespread. Usually parents cite

Messy Reading

Happen to need some inspiration in the Messy Department? Here are some messy books for your reading and mess-making pleasure:

Dirty Beasts by Roald Dahl

The Dirty Cowboy by Amy Timberlake

Cook a Doodle Doo by Janet Stevens

Cows in the Kitchen by June Crebbin

Harry the Dirty Dog by Gene Zion

I Like Getting Dirty/Me Gusta Ensuciarme by Rosa Sarda

Mrs. Wishy-Washy by Joy Cowley

Mud by Mary Lyn Ray

Tom and Pippo Make a Mess by Helen Oxenbury

Warthogs Paint - A Messy Color Book by Pamela Duncan Edwards

that it is because they are concerned about their child's health and safety or, if indoors, the "safety" of their furniture and other household items. More often than ever before, many children never get the chance to get messy indoors.

Indoors or out, we must provide children with opportunities to explore with materials freely and to get dirty in order to help them construct knowledge and ultimately creative thinking. Here are a few great sensory experiences conducive to a good old-fashioned constructive mess:

MUD

See a few drops of rain hit the window and, for many children, it is all over. Forget the raincoats. Forget the boots. They shoot out the door, barefoot and at lightening speed, straight to a favorite place: mud dripping through fingers, the exploration of how much dry dirt it takes to get the right consistency, and the continuous patting of that incomparable gooey substance is the quintessential sensory mess. Provide pie tins, funnels, molds, sticks (which make great candles!), leaves, stones, and other natural materials for a truly creatively muddy experience. Even if you have to get the hose out before the kids come in and then carry them to the tub, there is nothing like a good old-fashioned mud pie to get the creative juices flowing!

WATER

Perhaps the easiest mess to clean up, and one of the most wonderful to explore, is water. Try setting up a car, bike, or garden tool "wash." Turn a small child's pool into the washing area and you might get your own self-contained mud area. Explore with things that float and sink. See what kind of tools will make the most inventive spray. Add paint brushes to the scene. Add some glycerin and soap and let them explore and get messy with bubbles and their own invented bubble blowers. Don't forget to rinse off.

COOKING

Now that the kids have gotten good and messy in the mud and water, let them try it in the kitchen. Exploring in the kitchen is a great way for kids to get a truly sensory experience. Do your best to let go of any anxieties about a clean kitchen space, if only for a moment. Let your kids try these tools, techniques, and explorations in the kitchen:

Dough

Allow children to experiment with different types of ingredients for dough. Use all types of flour, cornstarch, and corn or nut meal. Add textured ingredients like cooked rice, oatmeal, and raisins. See how much liquid you need to get the desired result. Get sticky. Make shapes. Knead. Knead. Knead.

Yeast Experiments

Provide a package of yeast and just let your children explore. If they haven't already been introduced to it, talk to your children about what yeast needs to do its "work." Tell them the yeast wants to grow, but like us it needs food (sugar and warm water). Try it with cold water and then experiment with other substances such as warm milk. See what happens.

Countertop Fun

- Explore with flour or salt in a tray or on the counter—it's amazing what fun a few cars, some fingers or other "tools" can bring to a pile of flour on the kitchen table.

- Place a stool in front of the kitchen sink and allow exploration. If you can place a tub inside the sink, it will save water.

- Squeeze juice.

- Rinse and tear lettuce. This is tons of fun even if your salad isn't quite as uniform as you like it.

- Make breadcrumbs or a cracker crumb crust by adding a little bit of melted butter to crumbs. Experiment with creative ways to make crumbs (in a grinder or mortar and pestle, with a rolling pin in a plastic bag, or crumbling with hands).

- Grind and grate to your heart's delight! Let your children try their hand at grating carrots, cucumbers, and cheese. If you have a mortar and pestle, allow them to grind up seeds (such as coriander or cumin) or pieces of crackers.

See Chapter 13, *Thinking Outside the Recipe*, for more ideas about cooking with kids.

ARTISTIC MESSES

Art projects and art exploration are natural means of constructive messes. Papier-mâché, sculpture, collage, and paint are great ways to let kids get their messies out. See sidebar for recipes.

See Chapter 14, *Art Smart*, for more ideas related to developing creativity through the arts.

Fun Messy Recipes

Cloth Sculpture

This recipe makes fun sculptures that dry very hard.

1-1/2 cups Plaster of Paris
1 cup water
cloth, paper towel, or old sheet or other material

Mix the ingredients together until they are creamy.
Dip the cloth into the mixture.
Shape the cloth over recycled materials of your choice (bottle, tubes, wire, milk cartons) or make freeform, abstract sculptures.

Papier-mâché

Mix together 1 part glue and 1 part water.

Dip dryer lint, newspaper, or colored tissue paper strips into the glue mixture and gently lay them onto an inflated balloon, a bowl, or another object of your choice. Let your sculpture dry in a warm area for 2-3 days.

Nut Dough

1/2 cup nut butter of your choice
1/2 cup dry milk
1 T. honey or agave nectar, if desired for sweetness

Mix the ingredients together. Explore and, if your hands were clean when you began, eat!

Soap Dough

Mix 1 cup powdered detergent with 2 Tablespoons water and food coloring. Try beating it with an egg beater or other tools you might have. It will become shiny and stiff. This is great exploration before the water runs in the bathtub, or done on a tray over the kitchen sink.

Goop

1 1/2 cups very warm water
2 cups white glue
A few drops of food coloring and/or glitter
1 1/3 cups very warm water
2 teaspoons Borax

Mix 1-1/2 cups very warm water, the glue, and food coloring and/or glitter together thoroughly.

In a separate bowl, mix together 1 1/3 cups very warm water and the Borax.

Add the Borax mixture to the glue mixture and combine thoroughly. You can explore for days with this mixture if it is kept in an airtight container.

Ooblek!

Add 1 cup of water and a few drops of food coloring to a box of cornstarch. This makes an intrinsically interesting (and messy) substance with which to experiment.

Bath Paints

This also makes great and easy-to-clean window paint. Pour 1 part tempera paint and 1 part liquid dish soap together in a bottle and shake it vigorously until mixed. Use bath paints to explore in the tub!

CLEAN MESSES

Not all messes create havoc; some messes are clean. Have a dirty table? A toothpaste splattered mirror? Make a mess to get it clean! Explore with shaving cream or some very lathery soap bubbles on a tabletop or mirror. Don't forget a few favorite sponges or wash rags and possibly a squeegee to help along that creative exploration. Add some color to shaving cream for extra messy fun. If you can take the table outside, let your children explore with hosing it down as a grand finale.

A PLACE FOR EVERYTHING, EVEN MESSES

"But I have such a hard time seeing messes all over the house," you say. Or, perhaps there is just always a mess and you feel like you are drowning in all the clutter that seems to pile up. It doesn't mean you need to give up providing sensory experiences for your children. Perhaps you just need some ideas for containing messes:

Project Table

Allow for a table that never (or at least rarely) needs to be cleaned up. If the sight of the messy table bothers you, designate it in a lesser-seen area of your home, but not so far out of sight that it doesn't get played with often.

Creativity Corner

Designate a corner of your house or yard where the kids know it is okay to be messy, and where they can leave a mess from day to day, and rediscover later. As hard as it may be for you, try to resist the temptation to pick up those scattered Legos™ or the train track that runs from the bathroom to the living room. Being able to return to a project even days later can do wonders for the creative process.

Bathtubs!

Worried about finger paints getting on Grandma's old table? Bring those messy materials into the bathtub; it's a great place for any messy project even if there is no water involved.

Outdoors

If all else fails, be messy outdoors. Even paint washes or wears away on outdoor surfaces; grass is a great place to get out messy materials. After-rain puddles make the best messes!

Mess Effect

The reason often stated for not allowing children to fully explore and get messy is that parents are uncomfortable with cleaning up. When beginning a messy-prone project, preparation for the mess will make it easier to accept. Lay down newspapers for easy cleanup. Dress children in "play" clothes or allow your child to use messy material without any clothes. Use smocks, tarps, or an old tablecloth or sheet to protect your work surface. Pull hair back, remove shoes, or put on rain boots if appropriate. Before getting messy together, talk about what clean up will look like. Know that the more you get messy and go through the routine of cleaning up together, the easier the process will get.

Although it may be difficult at times to accept the messes our children (need to) make, know that you can. But don't just accept the mess, rejoice in it, knowing that you are supporting your child's creative growth even further.

Resources

The Big Messy Art Book: But Easy to Clean Up by MaryAnn F. Kohl

Making Sense of Art: Sensory-Based Art Activities for Children With Autism and Asperger Syndrome by Sandra Davalos

Mudworks by MaryAnn F. Kohl

Sand and Water Play: Simple, Creative Activities for Young Children by Sherrie West and Amy Cox

chapter 13

tHiNkiNg outside the recipe!

Using Cooking to Develop Creativity

We've been challenging ourselves and our children to think outside the box. Even with the best of intentions, we sometimes do things to inhibit the very curiosity we're trying to spark. Before we notice it, we catch ourselves falling into old patterns, telling our little ones to "color inside the lines" or "follow directions" on a worksheet. We focus more on the product than the process. This can easily be a limitation in the kitchen. Treating a recipe as sacred, it's easy to miss out on the fun and the learning.

When you talk about learning and the kitchen in the same sentence, many people instantly conjure up a picture of measurement, fractions, counting, volume, capacity, temperature, addition, subtraction, multiplication, and division. Those are all wonderful perks of cooking with children, but what about creativity?

Sure, we strive for the perfect banana bread. Having something to show for it gives our learning meaning. It becomes easy to strive ourselves right out of our innate sense of inquiry, the pure joy we accessed while digging in the mud or exploring texture while mouthing anything and everything as babies. As a result, we (often unintentionally) give up our wings.

One Super Easy Tortilla! (serves 1)

Stir 3T. Masa Harina (Tortilla Flour) with 2T. warm water and form the dough into a smooth ball.

Roll the dough between two damp cloths with a rolling pin to form tortillas.

Cook each tortilla about 2 minutes on a 400 degree griddle. Yum! Yum!

When children are given the opportunity to truly spread their wings in the kitchen, they are able to come to a new place in their creative development. Cooking allows children another way to connect with their world, explore natural materials, mimic real scientists, and learn ways to approach future problems and recipes. Being able to ask questions and make discoveries on their own is what will lead children to an understanding of their world. Even though science is logical, systematic, and objective, it is often only through the spirit of play and genuine curiosity that scientists solve problems most effectively.

When you enter the kitchen as a scientist, realize it is not just a place where *the box* (or recipe) must prevail. Realize that it can be the creative center of a home, and anything can happen there. The blender is a forgiving tool that accepts spinach, peanut butter, mangoes, and grains. A breakfast bar can hold bananas, jam, oats, yogurt, seeds and nuts, tofu, and whatever else the fridge or pantry offers. It is just like everything else in life: learning to find ways to work together (in this case, ingredients that work together) is an investigation into relationships.

In the precious little book *The Wise Woman and Her Secret* by Eve Merriam, a woman refuses to reveal the secret of her wisdom. A young girl finally discovers it: "The secret is to be curious . . . to keep on wandering and wondering." When exploring creativity, it is the wandering and wondering that we seek to nurture. Continuing to explore, finding more ways to think outside the recipe is one tool you can use to help your children get there. While not all of your kitchen explorations and exploits may be tasty, marching to the beat of your own recipe will truly provide the ingredients needed to cook up some good old-fashioned curiosity.

INQUIRING EATS: FOODS YOU CAN GET CREATIVE WITH

"I'm gonna need my chef hat for this!" my curly headed five year-old excitedly exclaimed carefully arranging his stool at the kitchen counter. A pinch of this. A smidgen of that. Cupfuls of shredded carrots, and scoops of raisins. Perhaps a helping of maple syrup and some nut butter. Throw in a boogie and his own vibrato of his new favorite song *Sammy the Dog Has Learned to Play Trombone!* Instant Energy Balls! It's his recipe, his timetable, his mess, his fun, and definitely his inquiry.

Pies and Crumbles

Experimenting with fruit and toppings is a great place to start with children in the kitchen. With or without a crust, let your kids throw together the fruit of their choice (apples, blueberries, cherries, peaches, blackberries, etc.) and top them with their own combination of grains (oatmeal, rice, flax, almond meal) and sweeteners (honey, molasses, agave nectar, brown rice syrup, Sucanat, etc.). Served warm or cold, this is a great way to help your child begin experimenting with his or her own combinations of foods.

Roll-ups!

Think sushi. Think burritos. Think way beyond the recipe here. Once you start making roll ups in your home, your kids will likely take off in their creative exploration of food. Use a tortilla, lavash bread (large flat bread) or a large green leaf (favorites are nori

"Some people like to paint pictures, or do gardening, or build a boat in the basement. Other people get a tremendous pleasure out of the kitchen, because cooking is just as creative and imaginative an activity as drawing, or wood carving, or music."
—Julia Child

Wonder Words

Personal Pizza and Pretzel Dough

This recipe makes a basic yeasted dough for 1 soft pretzel or personal sized pizza.

1/2	teaspoon yeast
4	teaspoons warm water
1/2	teaspoon oil
1/2	teaspoon honey
4	Tablespoons flour

Sprinkle the yeast over the warm water. Stir. Let the yeast dissolve until it forms a bubbly surface.

Stir in the oil, honey, and flour.

Knead the ingredients together on a lightly floured board. Cover dough with a cloth and let rise for about 20 minutes. Roll dough into a circle (for pizza) or use your hands to make "worms" (for pretzels).

For pretzels, drop shaped dough into boiling water for about 20 seconds or until it floats to the top of your water.

Place pretzel or personal pizza onto a greased cookie sheet. Add toppings. Bake for 8-10 minutes at 450 degrees.

sheets or chard and collard greens) and add whatever ingredients you have on hand. Try sliced carrots, cucumber, zucchini, sweet bell pepper sticks, apple slices, sprouts, rice noodles, beans, or cheese. Roll them together. Provide a dip like hummus or peanut sauce and you're good to go!

Salads

Salad greens are a common missing ingredient from the diet of children. Maybe it's the texture. Maybe the color. Regardless of the reason, salads are great to explore. Cut out the greens if that's the problem and see what your kids come up with for salad. Try shredded carrots and beets with raisins, or cucumbers, tomato,

"Cooking is like love, it should be entered into with abandon or not at all."

—Harriet van Horne

and avocados. Encourage them to try their own combinations without making judgments about what ingredients go together. Let them experiment with toppings: toasted pumpkin or sunflower seeds, sea vegetables, dried fruit, or their own homemade dressings. Even yogurt or cottage cheese are fun. Don't forget fruit salads, which are an easy way to let go of recipes, and an even better way to try some more exotic, non-traditional fruits.

Pizza! And Pretzels, Too.

Dough is the most wonderful way to get the creativity happening in the kitchen, and perhaps one of the easiest ways to start. Use the sidebar recipe to make single portions of pizza dough. Provide all the usual toppings and a few new ones and let everyone make their own dinner tonight. Use the same pizza dough recipe to let your kids make their own pretzel shapes. See what interesting pretzels they can come up with: letters, numbers, or crazy shapes.

Juice and Smoothies

Juice out that creativity! Because juicing and blending completely changes the form of any given food item, it's one of the most exciting ways for kids to explore with a variety of ingredients. Smoothies, especially, are a great way to get creative in the kitchen! See the article insert for some super smoothie ideas!

Cookies

Once your children have explored with ingredients that work well together and combinations of foods they enjoy, try letting them come up with their idea of what goes in the perfect cookie. Even very young children can do this. Brainstorm together what your child would like to put in his cookies and, without judgment, start combining. Let their ideas guide the process and see what happens.

Books About Cooking, Baking, and Making Messes in the Kitchen

Bread, Bread, Bread by Ann Morris

Bread Is for Eating by David Gershator

Cook-a-Doodle-Doo by Janet Stevens & Susan Stevens Crummel

Everybody Bakes Bread by Norah Dooley

Growing Vegetable Soup by Lois Ehlert

The Little Red Hen (Makes a Pizza) by Philemon Sturges

The Little Yellow Chicken by Joy Cowley

Pumpkin Soup by Helen Cooper

Sun Bread by Elisa Kleven

Too Many Cooks! by Andrea Bucklee and Marilyn Burns

The Tortilla Factory by Gary Paulsen

PLAY WITH YOUR FOOD: EXPERIMENTING IN THE KITCHEN

Now that you and your child are beginning to explore in the kitchen, take a look at all the neat things your food can do. From playing with cornstarch goo and swirling food colorings to watching yeast work, there are many great experiments you can do with food. See Chapter 18, *Lightbulb Moments,* for specific ideas for playing with your food.

GET MOTIVATED

If you think your children aren't interested in cooking, try these ideas for getting and keeping them motivated in the kitchen:

Masquerading

By using chef hats and aprons, you make it official and bring all the fun of pretend play to your kitchen. Cooking clothes are found readily at toy stores, but consider making your own with some fun cooking-themed material or scraps leftover from last year's Halloween costume. Check restaurant supply stores for more official-feeling chef wear.

My Own Utensils

Have a set of measuring spoons and other utensils set aside just for your child. Search garage sales, dollar stores, or flea markets for interesting cooking tools. Some wonderful utensils for children to explore with are apple corers/peelers/slicers, can openers, chopsticks, hand mixers, nut grinders, and pastry bags for decorating.

Publish Your Successes

Allow your child to create his or her own "favorites" cookbook. Keep a notebook in your kitchen designated for writing down your child's favorite recipes and creations as they are made. Include ideas for magic potions (combinations of foods that are not meant to be eaten) as well as what goes in their favorite smoothies, salads, and cookies. Perhaps your child's favorite food is a Sauce Sandwich (just bread and a favorite sauce). Take dictation for the directions to make it. Type up the recipes and post them in your kitchen or keep them in protective sleeves for future use. Use drawings, photos, or stickers to decorate your recipes, then bind them all together.

Continue to refer back to your child's recipes often; the repetition will build independence, reinforce process and measurement vocabulary, and boost self-esteem.

Get Messy

Instead of spoons, allow your chef to get messy and stir with her hands. It's amazing how much better food tastes when it is mixed this way. Don't forget to wash your hands first, roll up your sleeves, and then, if you haven't used eggs in your cooking (uncooked they can carry salmonella), clean your hands, the bowl, or spoon with the best cleaning tool, your tongue.

A Word About Single Portion Cooking

Perhaps the best thing to motivate our young chefs is to allow them to work through an entire recipe by themselves. Rather than just being involved through a bit of pouring, mixing, and lots of watching, children take charge of their cooking experience while they measure, mix, cut, pour, grind, mold, and knead all themselves. It's fairly easy to take your family's favorite recipes and make a single portion recipe by just halving and then halving again until you get one serving.

Act it Out

Experiment with acting out your creations and processes. Whatever actions you come up with will deepen your child's experience and understanding of cooking. While the bread is baking, act like yeast. What would happen to you if we added a bit of sugar and warm water? Work, yeast, work! Pretend to be oozy cheese melting. Pretend to be the toast in the toaster and "pop!" Even pretend to milk the cow before opening the fridge. What does the oil do when it is starting to heat up in the pan? How about boiling water?

Shop Together

Shopping for ingredients together introduces nutrition, categorization, consumer awareness, denominations of money, making change, and writing lists. You'll never know what new and interesting things your child might decide to try when they are involved in the choices.

Be safe, healthy, and enjoy some good home cookin' together. The next time you hear, "Hey Mom! Can you get that mixing bowl down for me?" Let yourself allow your children to think outside the recipe. Now off to the lab you go!

Totally Smoothie!

"Let's make it GREEN!" My son joyfully squealed while tossing a handful of fresh organic spinach atop bananas, rice milk, peaches, and almond butter into the family blender. Liquefy. Stir. Chop. Pulse. "Green Smoothie!" he cried out in celebration, jumping up and down on his stool. His delight is truly scrumptious, as is his breakfast.

Oh, the magic of the blender, the most forgiving tool in our busy lives and kitchens today. Getting our toddlers and young children to eat their share of whole fruits and veggies (or even any at all) can sometimes be a struggle. Spending some time getting to know smoothies may help your young child get those much-needed nutrients, with the added bonus of being a way to connect with your kids and spark creative fun in the kitchen.

Smoothies offer a way to meet your child's daily whole foods quota. Reports by the *Journal of the American Dietetic Association* show that toddler and young child consumption of dark, green, leafy vegetables has become increasingly low and that fewer than 10 percent of all infants and toddlers consume ANY green leafies in a given day. Whole fruits and other vegetables are increasingly absent from the diet of young children as well. Smoothies can be our baby-step personal solution to this national problem.

Via the all-amazing smoothie, the kitchen has the great potential to become your very own investigational lab. Use a smoothie to explore ways to get them to eat their veggies while providing an opportunity to problem solve ("It's too thick, what should we do?") and think outside the box, in this case, to think outside the recipe. Give ownership to the smoothie experience by allowing your child to get creative with what goes in it. She'll soon find out the joy of mixing colors and what it takes to make a purple, pink, green, orange, brown, or white smoothie. As you experiment with your blender, you'll likely find that there really isn't a need for recipes and you can feel confident that there isn't a more ideal way to encourage inquiry and exploration in your young children. With a smoothie, it is nearly impossible to fail. And it's the trial and error, like all things we learn, that will help us and our kids to become more in tune with our creativity and become better problem solvers.

Smoothies are a wonderful way for your family to take advantage of the many benefits of raw foods. "We can expose more nutrients by blending, pureeing, and juicing. This keeps the vitamins intact, as well as the enzymes, and accomplishes the goal of steaming without any loss of food value," says David Wolfe, CEO of rawfood.com and author of *Eating for Beauty*. "Juicing, blending, and pureeing is a way of breaking up fiber without corrupting by heat the integrity of the fiber itself, the nutrients contained in the plant cell, and the quality of the water in the food." When you turn on the blender, you instantly win half the battle by eliminating the texture of a new raw food while enjoying a nutrient rich meal.

Even the savviest little palate will often have difficulty identifying all the nutritious ingredients in a smoothie. Because veggies and other ingredients blend so nicely, the only evidence of their presence in a smoothie will sometimes be the color. So it is easy to get added doses of protein by adding nut butters, avocados, soft tofu, soy milk, or yogurt. Experiment with wheat germ, rice milk, and flax seed for added grains. Sneak in kale, spinach or other leafy greens, peas, pumpkin, squash, or tomato juice. Use soluble fibers such as oat bran or brown rice, and your own variation of favorite fruits such as berries, grapefruit, oranges, melons, peaches, pears, or pineapple. Add carrots, cucumber, cauli-flower, or zucchini. Complete your meal with an alternative to refined sweeteners like coconut milk, molasses, honey, or maple syrup, but realize that the perfect smoothie need not be sweetened up any more than the natural sweetness that the fruit provides. Sometimes just adding a bit of freshly squeezed beet or carrot juice, or rice or vanilla soy milk can be enough to sweeten a smoothie to your child's liking. Of course, before blending, make sure your child is not allergic to those hidden ingredients.

Smoothies are an all around perfect snack or meal for the young child. They are fast, convenient, affordable, satisfying, a tool to spark creativity, and let's not forget nutritious. So give it a whirl; energize your kids and yourself with a smoothie and devour those nutrients, along with the fun!

Resources

Cook and Learn by Barbara Veitch

Cook and Learn: Recipes, Songs, and Activities for Children by Adrienne Wiland

Cooking on a Stick: Campfire Recipes for Kids by Linda White

The Homeschool Cooking with Kids System in a Box by Laura Bankston

Learn Spanish in the Kitchen by Living Language

Learn French in the Kitchen by Living Language

The Kid's Campfire Book by Jane Drake and Ann Love

Storybook Stew by Suzanne I. Barchers and Peter J. Rauen

explore more!

Developing Creativity and Thinking Skills Through the Arts, Sciences, Stories, and Media

*persistent dreams
guide a stone's fall to
heaven*

chapter 14

Developing Creativity Through Visual Arts

"I saw the angel in the marble and carved until I set him free."
—Michelangelo

Art is an expression of oneself. While there are many definitions of art, this one encompasses our whole selves, our whole children and how they choose to express themselves. It is a voyage into oneself. Parents need not define themselves as "artists" to facilitate creative expression through art in the home. What is needed is an open mind, flexibility, and access to materials and styles.

LEARNING TO LOOK

Young children move through their days with such passion and fervor that it is often a skill for a child of this age to pause and just observe. Learning to look is the first step to being able to develop creative expression through art.

Observing Art

From prehistoric works of art (rock carvings and cave paintings of the Cro-Magnon) to Egyptian hieroglyphs to African and Asian art and modern day marvels, regardless of the age of your children, experience art history together. Talk about how art has changed over time, look for similarities and differences in time periods and across cultures. What is unique? What types of materials were used? Especially interesting to children is looking at color, line, animals, nature, transportation, how movement is depicted, and representations of other children. They all lend themselves well to the direct experiences and interests of many young children.

Critiquing Art

To critique is to look carefully and analyze something, and then articulate feelings about it. It is clear that children begin to develop likes and dislikes early on in life. As you expose your child to different styles and observe art together, discuss concepts such as line, color, shape, space, and patterns. While many art critics spend time finding fault in artwork, when observing and discussing it with your children it does not need to be overtly negative, or negative at all. Discuss what the piece makes them feel, what they like about a piece, and of what it reminds them. If they don't prefer the piece, ask them to tell you why and then find one that does appeal to them.

MODELING ARTISTIC EXPRESSION

"I can't draw," said Kelly, mother of a three year-old. It may be true that you feel apprehensive about your own skills as an artist. Don't let your own artistic inhibitions prevent you from providing examples of creative expression through art. After all, what does "I can't draw" mean in the world of a child? And where does this come from? What does this teach a child? There is no "I can't" if judgment is reserved.

As previously discussed, having an example of creativity is vital in developing the creative spirit. So even if you are not creating art daily, provide opportunities for children to regularly experience it.

The Real McCoy

Keep art alive and exciting! Go to galleries, museums, exhibits, and visit artists in their studios. Seek out an art mentor when your child wants more guidance or desires instruction or models of a certain technique or style such as pottery, stenciling, print making, or pencil drawing. Many cities also have public art. Some may have beautification plans in place employing local artists to make sculptures, paintings, murals or mosaics for street corners or city centers. Go on an art scavenger hunt in your town and visit as much real and live art as possible. As you explore the art in your area, look also at billboards and signage to find other unique forms of artistic expression.

In Print

While a jaunt to St. Petersberg, Chicago, Paris, or Xi'an would be a wonderful opportunity to view art, for most families, visiting some of the world's greatest artworks is not practical. In absence of the real thing, we turn to print.

Most libraries have a varied collection of good books about artists, for kids and adults, that show varied styles of art (sculpture, recycled, canvas paintings, multicultural, museum collections). Embrace coffee table style artisan books as well, as they can really get your creative juices flowing. If your goal is to give an art background to your children, you may want to shy away from craft books and focus on styles for a while. But don't stop there.

An easy and relatively inexpensive way to introduce kids to artistic expression is through beginning a postcard collection. Postcards usually come with a short explanation of the artist and the medium used. Collecting postcards is a wonderful way for children to not only be exposed to great works of art but also a build a nice art collection for their own enjoyment and reference.

The Internet offers us access to collections of artwork like never before. From the comfort of your own home you can instantly crawl through the caves of Ajanta and Ellora or tour the Louvre. Like most print versions, but especially when using the Internet to view artworks, it is difficult to really know what it is like to be in the presence of the piece. Be sure to explore interesting pieces further. What is the actual size of the piece? What was the medium? Why was it created? When? Where? By whom?

Still, one of the most astounding ways for kids to experience visual art is in the many exquisite children's picture books available today. They are the quintessential avenue for introducing young children to art. See the resources at the end of this chapter for titles of books that are beautifully illustrated and use a variety of media.

COMMENTING ON ART WORK

In *The Little Prince* by Antoine de Saint Exupéry, the young boy was nearly devastated when the adults looking at his picture of a boa constrictor eating an elephant only said, "That is a hat." As we offer more opportunity for children to create in unique ways, we must also recognize the impact of our comments on our children's self image and future expression through art.

What to Say

When children create art, they often want to show the product to their parents or caregivers. But do they really need us to tell them they have done a good job? If so, why? And what does "good job" tell them? It is natural for human beings to seek out validation for their work, but it is also important to examine how we respond to the ways in which they create. As a parent, you want to be able to give nurturing feedback about what your child has done. Be aware that reflexively saying "good job" does not give children any information about their work. As educator Alfie Kohn asserts, just saying "good job" can have a negative effect by making children praise dependent.

Giving specifics about something the child has done can be a valuable way of commenting on artwork. Offer statements such as:

"You are trying to come up with your own idea."

"I see you are trying new materials, techniques, etc."

"What an experiment to mix those colors in that way."

Encourage your child to become a more reflective and intrinsically motivated creator by asking questions that guide him in telling about what he has done. Ask questions about what materials and techniques he has used. Explore if there was anything about the process that was fun or especially challenging. See Chapter 4, *The Art of Questioning*, for more information about using questioning techniques to help children think reflectively, and Chapter 22, *Other Side of the Mountain*, for more about celebrating creativity.

Invoke Feelings and Make Connections

Relating art to real life and personal experiences is yet another way for children to not only experience the art but make meaning of it and take the experience deeper. Use the time you spend observing and making art together as an opportunity to tune in to prior experiences and learn about each other. Does it remind you of a time in your life when something funny or sad happened? What does it make you feel? Why do you think so? Why do you think the artist chose to use all those shades of red? Do you think the artist was feeling happy when she created this?

TIME FOR ART

While it is true that some children have predictable schedules for how they will act at certain times of the day, for very young children, it is often difficult to dictate when art is going to happen and when they will feel like creating in this way. If you sign a child up for an art class, there is no guarantee that she is going to feel like painting on Monday morning at 10 a.m. Consider making art time *anytime*, meaning that at least very simple art materials (such as the ones listed below) are always accessible to your young child.

ARTFUL EXPERIENCES

Drawing

Allow opportunities for drawing with many different tools such as pencils, crayons, chalk and pastels, charcoal, markers, and anything else you feel comfortable with your child using to experiment with drawing.

Painting

Use tempera paints, water colors, and finger paints. Provide many sizes and types of brushes for children to experiment with. Beyond brushes, look towards other items you can paint with. Paint with old windshield wipers, sponges, rags, potatoes, coffee filters, feathers, and straws. If painting feels stress-inducing for you, see Chapter 12, *Squish! Splat! Smoosh!*, for ideas about containing messes.

Sculpture

Provide children with intriguing sculpture and modeling opportunities. Use earth clay, homemade dough, plasticine, and papier-mâché (see Chapter 12, *Squish! Splat! Smoosh!*, for a recipe). Many wonderful ideas and recipes for modeling and carving experiences can be found in the resources at the end of this chapter. But don't stop there. Use wire and foil or other recycled materials. Experiment with sculpture by using food to create sculptures of faces, animals, or buildings. Use your bodies, silverware, furniture, a pile of stones, and other commonly found items to make sculptures.

Construction

Construction is a valuable visual art experience for very young children. From as early as six months, children are interested in building towers, stacking objects, and exploring how things go together. Both two- and three-dimensional opportunities for construction are useful in developing understanding of the world and exploring creative expression. Use recycled materials (paper towel and toilet paper rolls, empty food containers, cereal boxes) and construction toys to allow the creation of buildings and other structures.

"I found I could say things with color and shapes that I couldn't say any other way...things I had no words for."
—Georgia O'Keefe

Mixed Media

Collage and mixed media are a wonderful way for young children to experiment with combinations. Allow children to add layers to their painting with other items. Make collages of natural materials. Use magazines and photos to put ideas together. Add words that your child finds meaningful.

SETTING UP YOUR ART AREA

As children become comfortable with art materials, art becomes a communication tool and a true medium for expression. Having a place in your home designated for art and art supplies integrates it into everyday life. It provides many more opportunities for art whenever the muse strikes rather than just because it is *art time*.

Define Your Space

The space in which you do art could be anywhere in your home. One family spoke of having an extra room in the house (imagine that!) designated as the art room. It is a space they never need to clean up so tables, materials, easels and paints are always left out. Another family I know has their art supplies always available and set up in their very cozy basement. At a place we once lived, we had our garage set up as the art place. But keep in mind that it doesn't have to be an entire room. An art corner will do. Just make it a place where your family members can have access to it at all times. Even if that means they simply have to open a cupboard to get to it.

Consider your space and the possibility of having designated working surfaces such as drop down tables or easels. Adding a plastic drop cloth or an old sheet can instantly transform any room into an art studio. Having access to a sink either directly in or near to your art area is especially helpful when using messier media such as paint. Consider also creating a portable art area such as a tub or box of supplies, which can easily be packed up for outdoor use or to take on travels.

Take Your Time

Start small and build up your space over time. If you set up an art area and put twenty new types of supplies in it all at once, you are likely to overwhelm your little artist. Some supplies you may want to add to your art area over time could be:

- recycled materials (toilet paper rolls, old boxes, milk cartons, bubble wrap, yogurt containers, wallpaper samples, wire pieces, old maps)
- feathers
- all types of glue—glitter, white, wood, and glue sticks
- clay (not just playdough, but actual earth clay)
- clay tools (real clay tools and other "tools" like plastic knives, chopsticks, etc.)
- items to trace (stencils or shapes cut from cardboard)
- stamps (the kind used for batiking work well with regular paint or finger paint)
- different kinds of paint—tempera, watercolors, finger paints, acrylic (for clothes or other permanents)
- old calendars, magazines, newspaper clippings, and cards —these make for great cutting and gluing projects.
- different kinds and sizes of scissors—straight edge, squiggly edges, etc.
- blank books to be filled on the child's own or together as part of storytelling or scrapbooks
- stickers
- body paint
- raffia and ribbons
- corks (that can be used for "pointillism" type paintings or other experimenting)

- chalk/chalkboard
- oil pastels
- pipe cleaners
- rolling pins
- items from your Nature Table (see Chapter 3, *Breaking Ground*)

See the resources at the end of this chapter for great places to buy supplies.

Name Your Space

Naming your space will give ownership and a sense of pride to those using it. Give your studio space a name like "Sally's Studio" or "Al's Art Area." Make signs together like "Creations Made Here" or "I create!" to adorn your area. They will evoke a sense of pride, joy, and awareness of the process.

Gather Together

Art does not have to be a solo flight. Set up an art club where a few young artists can scribble and create together. Have gallery openings of your own and invite your family and friends. Enjoy the act of creation and expression together!

Resources

Picture Books with Exquisite Artwork

The Big Big Sea by Martin Waddell, Illustrated by Jennifer Eachus

Eric Carle's Animals Animals compiled by Laura Whipple, Illustrated by Eric Carle

Hattie and the Wild Waves by Barbara Cooney

Island Boy by Barbara Cooney

The High Rise Glorious Skittle Skat Roarious Sky Pie Angel Food Cake by Nancy Willard, Illustrated by Richard Jesse Watson

King Bidgood's in the Bathtub by Audrey Wood, Illustrated by Don Wood

The Last Dance by Carmen Agra Deedy, Illustrated by Debrah Santini

Life Doesn't Frighten Me at All by Maya Angelou, Illustrated by Jean Luc
  Basquiat

I Live in Music by Ntozake Shange, Illustrated by Romaire Bearden

The Magic Paintbrush by Robin Muller

The Tale of the Mandarin Ducks by Katherine Paterson, Illustrated by Leo &
  Diane Dillon

Wild Child by Lynne Plourde, Illustrated by Greg Couch

Picture Books about Art

Art Auction Mystery by Anna Nilsen

Art Fraud Detective by Anna Nilsen

The Art Lesson by Tomie dePaola

Can You Find It?: Search and Discover More Than 150 Details in 19 Works of Art
  by Judith Cressy

*Can You Find It, Too?: Search and Discover More Than 150 Details in 20 Works of
  Art* by Judith Cressy

Draw Me a Star by Eric Carle

The Great Art Scandal: Solve the Crime, Save the Show! by Anna Nilsen

I Am An Artist by Pat Lowery Collins

The Lion and the Little Red Bird by Elisa Klevin

Maze: A Riddle in Words and Pictures by Christopher Manson

Purple, Green and Yellow by Robert Munsch

Terry's Creature by Deborah Gould

Resources for Discovering Art with Your Children

Animals in Art (National Gallery Series) by Ljiljana Ortolja-Baird

The Art Book For Children by Editors of Phaidon Press

Cave Paintings to Picasso: The Inside Scoop on 50 Art Masterpieces by Henry M.
  Sayre

Child's Play: Easy Art for Preschoolers by Leslie Hamilton

Come Look With Me: Animals in Art by Gladys S. Blizzard

Discovering Great Artists by MaryAnn F. Kohl

I Spy a Lion: Animals in Art by Lucy Micklethwait

Leonardo da Vinci for Kids: His Life and Ideas, 21 Activities by Janis Herbert

Monet and the Impressionists for Kids: Their Lives and Ideas, 21 Activities by Carol Sabbeth

Shadow Play: Making Pictures With Light and Lenses by Bernie Zubrowski

Young at Art: Teaching Toddlers Self-Expression, Problem-Solving Skills, and an Appreciation for Art by Susan Striker

Places to Buy Art Supplies

NASCO
www.enasco.com
800-558-9595

Lakeshore Learning Materials
www.lakeshorelearning.com
800-421-5354
Call for a catalogue.

chapter 15

jUMp, jiggLe, jive

Creative Explorations in Movement

"Jump! It's not as wide as you think."
— Joseph Campbell, giving advice to a young
Native American boy at his initiation

From the womb, movement has always been a part of us. For anyone who has ever watched a baby be calmed while swaying on his mother's hip, or a two year-old bounce up and down or back and forth, there is no denying that children are inspired by and respond to movement.

To many, it is no surprise that movement is a wonderful creativity developer and outlet. It offers children a way to express themselves, to make their own way with many possible answers, and to take risks with their learning. Simply put, movement offers children a solid beginning in practicing the *jump* they will so often need in their lives. In this chapter, you will find the importance of movement and its connection to learning, ways to move with your children, and how to help them use movement as an expression tool.

WHY EXPLORE MOVEMENT?

Movement is natural; it keeps us healthy and connected to living fully. Whether a child can be described as a kinesthetic learner or not, movement is a significant factor for learning. Paul Dennison, Ph.D., educator and kinesiology researcher, found that when movement was dramatically decreased in children ages 3-17, there was an increase in learning disabilities and performance on standardized tests was dramatically affected.

Movement has been described as the ultimate brain connector, and by moving we can eliminate stress, increase use of both hemispheres of the brain, think more clearly, and develop creativity.

EXPRESS YOURSELF

Being creative and expressing oneself go hand in hand. Movement offers children a way to express themselves in unique and positive ways; they don't need words, and there is no competition. Movement exploration is success- and creativity-oriented. Through movement, expression can happen in a variety of ways.

Climbing

Adventures in climbing offer a way for children to use their bodies in ways that are unique to other types of moving. Luckily, there are many options for children to develop the vertical movement that only climbing can offer. Provide opportunities for children to climb man-made items such as different types of ladders and ropes. As long as it does not impede others from coming down, don't be afraid to allow a child to climb *up* the slide! If they can figure out how to, let them climb even the walls, which in itself takes its own special skill. Many cities now offer indoor and outdoor rock climbing walls and will allow even young children to be attached to climbing equipment. Make sure your child also experiences climbing on natural objects such as varying sizes of rocks, sandy hillsides, and trees (see *How to Climb a Tree* in Chapter 8, *Wonder World*).

Put on Your Thinking Cap

In order to get ready for thinking, listening, or speaking, rub your ears from inside out and top to bottom. It will help you to listen, pay attention, and remember.

Dancing

Moving our bodies to music can be the most freeing of all sorts of movement. It offers opportunity to move all parts of the body from the tips of the toes to the top of the head. With dance, kids can wiggle, bounce, shake, squirm, and slide. With the exploration of the body in mind, dance has no limits or boundaries. Can you dance low? High? Slow? Quick? What are the different ways you can tap your toes? Try isolating your different body parts while you move to the music. Move just your shoulders. Can you move only your hips? Your diaphragm? How about just your eyes?

Explore all styles of dance, including hip-hop, square dance, belly dance, classical dance, synchronized dance, line dance, and other cultural dances. Try dancing to all types of music: jazz, blues, rock, country, classical, funk, soul, folk, and salsa. See the resources located at the end of Chapter 16, *Music in Me, Me, Mee!*, for great music to dance to.

Yoga

Yoga, the form of movement and breathing as a way of healing the body, dates back thousands of years and literally means "to be in union." Exploring yoga with children can help bring into union all the functions of the body and mind: strength, flexibility, balance, overall health, clear thought, productivity, and creative thinking. While it is useful to take a yoga class in order to understand many of the poses and breathing exercises associated with this age-old practice, there are also many resources available for you to explore and learn from. To begin familiarizing yourself and your children with yoga, draw pictures or find good simple pictures of some of the names of the poses. For example, find mountain, tree, butterfly, cobra, and lion pictures. Talk about the pictures and what you might be able to do with your body to simulate the animal or object pictured. Allow your child to make up new poses or names for poses. A pose by any other name is just as beneficial.

As you become more familiar, incorporate games, tell stories, and remain flexible (no pun intended)–allow your kids to create their own yoga program and just go with the flow!

Brain Gym®

The brain is processing tens of thousands of bits of new information each minute. In order to be working so hard, the brain cannot effectively do it alone; it needs movement to help it with that processing. Development experts Dr. Paul and Gail Dennison describe human brain function in terms of three dimensions: *laterality*, the two sides of the brain connecting; *focus*, the back and front of the brain connecting; and *centering*, the top and bottom of the brain connecting. When movements are made that stimulate all parts of the brain (left, right, front, back, top, and bottom), the brain can do its work easier. Through the Dennison's Brain Gym® program, children (and the adults supporting them) learn what movements support reading, writing, thinking, self-awareness, and study skills. Key components in Brain Gym® is that children have water regularly and find the best rhythms and timing for their learning.

Tiny Movements

When we speak about creative movement, people often refer to the large, or gross motor, movements children make. But there is also great potential in the power of all the tiny, or fine motor, movements. Play with the special movements of the fingers. Can your fingers tell a story? Explore with sign language and see the power of the hands to communicate. Perhaps even encourage your child to create their own hand signs for often used family sayings, a favorite or stuffed animal, or other signals that can communicate your child's needs. Bring focus to all the other tiny movements that our bodies can do. How can your toes move? What unique things can the elbows working together do? Can you wiggle your ears? How about just your nose? What does it take to connect with moving your eyebrows?

Cross the Midline

To connect the different sections of the brain, draw large infinity symbols in the air with your finger or paper streamers. You can also activate the brain by walking in place, lifting opposite arms and knees high. Touch the opposite hand to knee. Try doing it all to music and different rhythms.

Guided Imagery

Guided imagery, stories that require the listener to create pictures in their mind, help children to be more focused on specific movement and give their movements meaning. Guided imagery can be used for active movement times involving fast, upbeat, and rhythmic music, or during quiet settling times when you want to focus on relaxing tones and simple movements.

Tell about a leaf that has fallen from a tree, imagine what it encounters along the way, and move the way it might move. Does it hit the ground? A babbling brook? A raging river? How long does it take? What is the journey on the way down like? Stories about animals in the jungle, ones on the farm, or perhaps the adventures of a favorite lost hat are all ways to get your child moving in expressive ways. At the same time, telling stories and using guided imagery is a way for parent and child to connect on a deeper emotional level and express themselves together.

Trust Movement

Trust exercises have been used for decades as a way to develop communication skills, mutual respect, and teamwork. As a movement tool, trust exercises can help your child also learn to use their movements in a more sensory-heightened way. Some simple trust exercises you can try with young children include: falling backwards into an adult's arms, walking while standing back to back, or walking blindfolded while being physically or verbally guided around a room, through an obstacle course, or in a natural setting.

Moving Breath

While movement is often thought of as involving just body parts, we cannot ignore the breath and its role in the body. The air we breathe is what gives those movements life. Exploration with the breath and how it moves through the body is an important way to connect deeper with the functions of each body part and focuses those movements internally. Can you inhale and exhale slowly and deeply? Can you blow out with quick, short, and intense breaths? Can you fill your belly up like a balloon? How about give your favorite stuffed animal a ride on your belly? Can you make waves for it to surf? Try breathing in through only one nostril at a time, filling your lungs up as much as you can, and seeing if you can feel breath in various parts of your body.

Movement Solutions

With movement, children discover through experimentation and exploration and learn to find solutions. While imitation is widely used as a traditional teaching device, children need to be involved in divergent thinking opportunities that offer many possible responses and solutions. If the goal is creativity, self-expression, and problem solving, we must allow them to have choice in their expression, not merely imitations.

In this way, games, which seem a natural way to incorporate movement into a child's life, take on new meaning. When playing games like Red Light, Green Light, challenge children to stop in their favorite yoga pose. When dancing freely around the living room, ask them to show you how small they can get or to demonstrate a position that makes them feel glorious. Use verbal cues instead of demonstration to help children find a way to solve the problem you have posed instead of just copying what you have done. Likewise, make statements instead of correcting children's expressions through music and movement: "Wow! You are turning very slowly." Remember, there is no right or wrong way to move when it is an expression of oneself.

When children practice and learn to solve problems, the result is increased confidence. Since they have been involved in a learning process that has had them take ownership of their own responses, they discover an inner self-esteem and responsibility that will follow them to future creative ventures and areas of expression in their lives.

Moving Around the Furniture

Most agree that movement is a wonderful way to enhance a child's thinking, expression, and creativity. Still, we often require children to sit and listen, or ask them to stay still while we speak to them. Allowing a child to stand on her head while telling you a story, bounce on the furniture while you go over the plan for your day, or fiddle with some paperclips while you are discussing a problem could contribute to the child being able to process the information in more meaningful and concrete ways.

Movement Models

Just like any other building block of creativity, children need to see and experience other people and objects creating movements. In that regard, do your exercising in the presence of your children occasionally. Allow children the freedom to follow along with your own exercise routines if and when they so desire. Get your kids their own yoga mat and set it up near yours when you do yoga. You may find that they wish to join in everyday or just for part of your own routine. Try beginning your day with family movements that get you ready to take on the day such as breathing exercises and other movements listed in this chapter. After dinner, put on your favorite music and dance freely. Wind down together with slow, calming movements that prepare your body for rest such as simple stretches and curling and uncurling the body.

So, go ahead, jump, jiggle, and jive your way into movement. Jump into your creative expression. "It's not as wide as you think."

Tips to Help You Get a Move on

Introduce the Building Blocks of Movement

It's easy to take for granted all the little movements that make up our bigger bodily expressions. Bring awareness to the building blocks of movement by pointing out, separating, and then putting back together the different ways our bodies can move:

- Body moves: stretch, bend, twist, swing, sway, shake
- Body parts: head, shoulders, arms, hands, hips, back, feet, toes, etc.
- Direction: forward, backward, sideways, in and out, up and down
- Force: strong, sharp, smooth, tight, loose
- Level: high, low, and everything in between
- Shape: can you make a design with your body?
- Size: big, small, and everything in between
- Steps: walk, run, slither, jump, leap, gallop, slide, skip
- Tempo: fast, slow

Start Simply

Don't try to incorporate or learn too many movements all at once. Begin by just doing a few, and then adding another each time you move. Keep coming back to the ones you have already introduced.

Use Props

Props offer children new ways to express themselves. Use pinwheels, crepe paper or ribbon streamers, hoops, balloons, scarves, yarn balls, parachutes (see Chapter 10, *Hold My Hand*), tarps, or blankets to observe and talk about the movements each prop makes. Consider investing in a *shape changer*, a stretchy sack usually made of Lycra® material that allows creative movement and spatial exploration.

Observe Everyday Movement

The opportunity to see movement presents itself to us each day. Point out everyday movement to your children to get them more aware of how things move while learning new movement vocabulary:

Outdoors—wheels *turning*, brakes *squeaking*, leaves *falling*, wet dog *shaking*, horse *galloping*, cat *stretching*, trees *swaying*, kids *swinging*, merry-go-round *spinning*

At home—cap *twisting*, broom *leaning* and *swishing*, contents of a blender *whirling*, popcorn *popping*, pipe cleaners *bending*

Movement Resources

Picture Books and Read Alouds

Arches to Zigzags by Michael J. Crosbie

Brain Gym Surfer by Sandra Hinsley and Linda Conley

Cloud Dance by Thomas Locker

Edu-K for Kids by Paul E. Dennison, Ph.D., and Gail Dennison

Giraffes Can't Dance by Giles Andreae

Jamberry by Bruce Degen

Mountain Dance by Thomas Locker

My Mama had a Dancin' Heart by Libba Gray Moore

Water Dance by Thomas Locker

Video Resources for Moving with Your Kids

Animal Yoga for Kids by Sweet Productions

The Body in Motion by Discovery Communications

Curious Buddies. Let's Move! by Paramount

The Hidden Treasure by Creative Dance Adventures

Little Kicks: Fitness Workout for Kids Vol. 1& 2 by Bright Minds

Moving Freely: A Creative Dance Class by Creative Choices

YogaKids by Gaiam

YogaKids 2 ABC's for Ages 3-6 by Gaiam

YogaKids 3 Silly to Calm by Gaiam

Yoga Kids for Ages 3-6 by Gaiam

Audio Collections for Moving with Kids

Bean Bag: Activities & Coordination Skills by Kimbo Educational

Brain Gym®: Music for Encouraging Young Children to Complete Brain Gym Movements by Tessa Grigg, Brian Ringrose, and Sandy Hazledine

Kids in Motion by Greg Scelsa

Moving with Mozart by Kimbo Educational

Toes Up, Toes Down by Kimbo Educational

Where is Thumbkin? by Kimbo Educational

Resource Books for Moving with Kids

Brain Gym by Paul E. Dennison, Ph.D., and Gail E. Dennison

Dancing Wheels by Patricia McMahon

Fly Like a Butterfly by Shakta Kaur Khalsa

Movement Stories for Young Children Ages 3-6 by Helen Landalf

Rhythm Road: Poems to Move to selected by Lillian Morrison

Smart Moves: Why Learning is Not All in Your Head by Carla Hannaford, Ph.D.

Yoga with Children by Mary Stewart and Kathy Phillips

chapter 16

Music in Me, Me, Mee!

Exploring the Creative Potential of Music

There is a *whoosh-whoosh* rhythm in the womb, a mother's heartbeat in perfect time: nature's drum. With the sense of touch, this internal drumming can be felt at just a few weeks gestation. Then, at ten weeks, hearing develops and the *ssh!* of Mama's blood reaches the ears. This, our first music, begins before we even open our eyes.

This perfect rhythm is such a potent and primitive force in our lives. Perhaps related, listening to and making music have been classified as "brilliant neurological exercises." As we have already discussed in earlier chapters, the brain has different areas that are activated with various aspects of thinking and doing. It is much too simplistic to divide those functions because the brain is interconnected and cooperative. The more we do to stimulate *all* parts of the brain, the more we can encourage verbal memory, spatial reasoning, and cognitive processing. Brain research concludes that there is a window of opportunity during early childhood when neurons can be connected and the brain can develop the ability to learn new languages, hear tones, think spatially, and internalize distinct strategies to solve problems. With that in mind, it is important to provide substantial opportunities for hearing and making music early in a child's life. Luckily, those opportunities are available in abundance.

KEEP LISTENING

Music professionals agree that the only way one can develop a love and appreciation for music is by listening to it. Unfortunately, with all that children's brains are processing in the way of advertisements, fast-paced visuals, and other stimuli aimed at young people, their ability to listen has been on a rapid decline. Parents can help develop a child's ability to listen, and really hear, by providing opportunities to hear many different types of sounds and tones, bringing awareness to sounds as we hear them, and by playing listening games.

Music as a Foreign Language

It is often thought that achievement depends on aptitude. Shin'ichi Suzuki, creator of the Suzuki Method, believed that all children have the aptitude. He asserted that the potential of a child to learn music can be likened to the ability of the child to learn his mother tongue.

Dr. Edwin Gordon, an expert in music learning theory agrees, stating "no child is without music aptitude." Just like a foreign language, it is essential that children hear various tones early and correctly in order for the brain to make the connections.

Music Models

When choosing and looking for music opportunities for children, find the balance between experiencing models of naturally occurring music (the rain tip-tapping on the roof, rushing rivers, and the rustling of the trees) and man-made music. Expose them to jazz, blues, folk, world music, reggae, opera, and other types of music. Contact with many different types of creative expression through music gives children a larger platform from which to jump into their own expression.

In conjunction with giving plenty of opportunities to listen to music, look also at various visual interpretations of music in either print, motion picture, or live theatrical performances. Some great places to start with children are representations

(available on video) such as Disney's *Fantasia*, Sergei Prokofiev's *Peter and the Wolf*, and the *Carnival of the Animals* by French composer Camille Saint-Saens.

Let yourself sing and dance around the house, in the car, or on a walk. Joyful, spontaneous breakout in song is a beautiful model! Point out everyday music and what sounds are to be heard by listening to rain, vehicle sounds, trees rustling, chipmunks chattering, construction sites banging, the hum of the air conditioner, and by playing listening games.

Listening Games

Listening games are not only fun to play, they help develop a child's ear for distinguishing sounds and keep them alert to different tones. Once you begin playing listening games, your repertoire for recognizing sounds will begin to grow. Listening games are especially wonderful because they can be played anywhere you go.

- Find Sounds. Hide a ticking clock or egg timer somewhere in the house and see if your ears can find it before it rings.

- Change Sounds. What do you hear if you cover your ears? Try changing the shape of your hands from flat to varying degrees of being cupped. Does the sound change? Of what does it remind you?

- Go on a Listening Walk. While on a walk, in the airport, in the park or other fun places you find yourself, challenge your children to spend a few minutes in silence. Then, share with each other the sounds you heard. Play again and try to listen for new, interesting sounds.

- Distinguish Sounds. Play *Name that Tune* with some of your child's favorite songs. Play only a few seconds and see if they can guess the song. When flipping through the radio, see if you can identify which instruments are being used.

- Record Sounds. Make recordings of common household sounds (dishwasher, bathtub being filled, door opening, or the dryer running) and then play them back for each other to see if you recognize each sound.

MAKING MUSIC

Music is a wonderful way to connect us with each other, our needs, our desires, and our expressions. As you begin to think about how you can further incorporate listening and making music into your daily life, take the opportunity to get in tune with each other. Explore the awareness of how music makes you feel and consider how and when you already use it in your daily life. What ways does your child use music already? What kind of music does he enjoy? How does his body react when certain types of music come on the radio? Does he enjoy live music? Does he have opportunities to make music spontaneously? How? As a family, do you have opportunities to make music together? From there, you will have further understanding of how you already use music. As you then evaluate how best to share future experiences with your child, continue looking at how you can make music together, in new ways, throughout your day. Explore with patterns you hear and make, the songs you sing, and all types of instruments.

Rhythm Patterns

Learning to recognize patterns is a life skill and the brain is designed to perceive and generate patterns. Allow children opportunities to not only hear, but also feel and make their own rhythm patterns. Join in the music. Drum, use shakers, or clap out the rhythm. Make rhythmic motions with your feet, head, and hands. If you desire, consider also adding a metronome (a device which keeps a steady beat or tempo), which have been found to also help focus children with attention difficulties.

Song Writing

When exposed to language and rhythms of all kinds, children are our most intuitive poets. Their spontaneous ability to play on words, to join them together, and to let go of conventions allows them a unique freedom when it comes to song writing.

Establishing routines with music is a key way to keep it flourishing. Making up your own songs is a great way to establish routines: use them to say hello and goodbye, or incorporate a *clean up* or *time to leave* song. When you are telling stories, add songs for your characters to sing. Songs can be used to excite, stimulate, teach, or soothe, so incorporate them during all types of activity. Innovate on favorite songs by changing the words to fit what you are doing. In no time, you will likely overhear your young ones lulling their stuffed mouse to a dreamy slumber with their own lullaby.

EXPLORATION WITH INSTRUMENTS

When children are beginning to make music, anything they can hit, pluck, or blow through does the trick. Give plenty of opportunity for the children in your lives to explore freely with instruments to learn first how different instruments work, what sounds they make, and then explore ways to change those sounds and tones.

Accompaniment

Musical accompaniment to stories is a wonderful outlet for creative expression. Use homemade or professional musical instruments to accompany or tell your favorite family stories. What soundtrack can you create to help convey the meaning in the story? Use high and low sounds to tell stories like *Where the Wild*

Protect Your Hearing

There has been a mismatch in the world our bodies were made for and the world we have created. Our ears are designed for detecting the movements of predators, and not for sticking tiny speakers and amplifiers into them. Just like we have, music has evolved and recording companies are making music louder and louder. Music and other sounds that are too loud (above 85 decibels) can damage the eardrum, and by age six, many children have some noise-induced hearing loss. It is often difficult to ask a child to wear earplugs, but parents can be proactive in the protection of a child's hearing by turning volume down on televisions and stereos. If your children use iPods or other portable music players, use headphones that do not go inside of the ear. Make sure you use earplugs or noise canceling headphones when around especially loud sounds such as a lawnmower.

Things Are by Maurice Sendak. What would the Wild Rumpus sound like? Can you find an instrument that sounds like how the sun feels today? See Chapter 19, *Tell Me a Story*, for more ideas in developing creativity through storytelling.

To Drum Upon

Drums are ever present in our lives, often in forms we are not even aware of. Anything you can tap or hit can be a drum with its own unique percussive sound. Drum upon pots and pans, buckets, crates, all shapes and sizes of boxes, and other storage materials. How does the pitch change with the different sizes? If you stuff things inside (such as cloth, paper, beans, or pebbles), how does the sound change? How does a large rug hung out on a line thump differently? The backs of chairs and the rungs of ladders are especially fun to experiment with.

Whistle Me a Tune

Wind instruments are all about the breath moving in, on top of, and through various objects. They are an easily accessible music

Musical Fingers and Jingles

Gather your fingerpaints and a large poster paper. With a generous squirt, turn up the music, and let your fingers do the dancing. Add some extra fun by placing your paper into a pan and rolling some jingle bells into the paint. Rotate the pan back and forth and watch as your jingles are etched in history.

exploration. But whistles can come from other places too. On windy days, place a microphone near trees that still have their leaves, or near your downspout. Try out different sized cracks in the windows and vents in your home.

String Play

Strings make up many types of instruments, from pianos to guitars. Use different types of string to get started and hear what happens. Try yarn, thick rope made from cotton and nylon, and also other items you can pluck such as rubber bands. Distinguish the unique sounds each one makes. Fishing line is very much like guitar strings and is a simple, inexpensive material for children to experiment with plucking, strumming, and striking.

Ready to Play

Store bought instruments are also fun and provide many opportunities to explore creative expression. Begin with a few favorites: egg shakers, ukuleles, tambourines, maracas, kazoos, bongos or other hand drums, harmonicas, bells, cymbals, a small button accordion, slide whistles, xylophones, and the classic recorder.

Explore other lesser-known instruments such as the Australian didgeridoo, gongs, a potato ocarina, zils, an ocean harp, bagpipes, thumb pianos, steel drums, marimbas, and other drums from around the world.

RECORDING MUSIC

As you expand your use of music as a tool for creative development, you may be inclined to record some of the musical treasures that emerge, as well you should. It is truly fascinating to hear your own voice played back at you, especially in the case of children who likely have not had the opportunity to hear themselves often. Children can record themselves with a simple cassette player, but if you have the capability, record the music into your computer. There, you can add it to videos, mix it together to make medleys, and make your own music CD's or music videos. Once you have a nice selection, throw a dance party with your child as the DJ.

Our lives begin with the natural music of the beating of our mother's hearts. The beautiful challenge is to keep listening. Let nature's perfect drum be your musical guide.

Wonderful Music for Kids

Recorded Music

A Child's Celebration of Dance Music by Music for Little People

Birds, Beasts, Bugs and Fishes (Little & Big): Animal Folk Songs by Pete Seeger

Catch That Train by Dan Zanes and Friends

Fidgety Feet by Steve Rashid

For Our Children: 10th Anniversary Edition by Various Artists

If Fish Could Sing. . . Celtic Songs for All Ages by Teresa Doyle

Jazz for Kids: Sing, Clap, Wiggle and Shake by Various Artists

Let's Play by Raffi

Mary Had a Little Amp by Various Artists

Nicky's Jazz for Kids by Various Artists

Putumayo's collections such as *World Playground, African Playground, Animal Playground, Latin Playground, Caribbean Playground,* and *Asian Dreamland*

Ralph's World collections by Ralph Covert

Reading Rainbow's Greatest Hits by Various Artists

Singin' in the Bathtub by John Lithgow

Smithsonian Folkways Children's Music Collection by Various Artists

Young Dancer by Monika Tusnad

Songbooks

De Colores and Other Latin-American Folk Songs for Children by José-Luis Orozco

Diez deditos: 10 Little Fingers & Other Play Rhymes and Action Songs from Latin America by Elisa Kleven

Favorite Songs from Jim Henson's Muppets by Jim Henson

The Library of Children's Song Classics by Amy Appleby, comp.

Rise Up Singing: The Group Singing Songbook by Peter Blood and Annie Patterson, eds.

Rodgers and Hammerstein Children's Songbook by Richard Rodgers and Oscar Hammerstein II

Music Picture Books

Africa Calling, Nighttime Falling by Daniel Alderman

Charlie Parker Played Be Bop by Chris Racksha

Ella Fitzgerald: The Tale of a Vocal Virtuoso by Andrea Davis Pinkney

Freddie the Frog and the Thump in the Night: 1st Adventure — Treble Clef Island by Sharon Burch, Deborah Watley, and Tiffany Harris

Freddie the Frog and the Bass Clef Monster by Sharon Burch and Tiffany Harris

I Live in Music by Ntozake Shange

The Jazz Fly by Matthew Gollub and Karen Hank

John Coltrane's Giant Steps Illustrated by Chris Raschka

Meet the Orchestra by Ann Hayes

Mole Music by David McPhail

Sing a Song of Popcorn published by Scholastic, Inc

The Philharmonic Gets Dressed by Karla Kuskin

The Nutcracker by Michael Hague

Where the Wild Things Are by Maurice Sendak

Zin! Zin! Zin! A Violin by Lloyd Moss

Illustrated Musical Nursery Rhymes

Hey, Diddle Diddle by Salley Mavor

I'm a Little Teapot by Iza Trapani

It's Raining, It's Pouring by Kin Eagle

The Itsy Bitsy Spider by Iza Trapani

Mary Had a Little Lamb by Iza Trapani

Oh Where, Oh Where Has My Little Dog Gone? by Iza Trapani

Old MacDonald Had A Farm by Pam Adams

Row, Row, Row Your Boat by Annie Kubler

Twinkle, Twinkle, Little Star by Iza Trapani

Resources for Buying Instruments and Other Music Making Materials

Kindermusik
http://www.kindermusik.com

Lark in the Morning
http://www.larkinthemorning.com

Music for Kids
http://www.musicforkids.com

Music For Little People
http://www.musicforlittlepeople.com

Remo Drums
http://www.remo.com

everyday Math Magic

Using Math to Develop Creative Thinking

Magic is elusive and hard to define. Many magicians use *tricks* or slight of hand to look like they have control over natural forces. They have learned the building blocks of their trade. Beginning with each tiny step, they practice it until it becomes natural, put it together with a stage presence including jokes or stories, and make a rabbit appearing from a hat seem easy and effortless. The performance usually ends with a wow-ed crowd saying "How'd you do that?"

Everyday math provides the same kind of experience. It turns what has the potential to be difficult, foreign, and spellbinding into a creative venture. By learning the most basic building blocks and practicing them until they become natural, exploration into math and the power it gives children is truly magical.

BRING MATH TO LIFE

If ever there was an all around creativity, problem solving, and thinking builder, it would be math. Unfortunately, many people feel they are not a *math-type*. Children struggling with math often get labeled and often give up on math. The math experienced is then painful and anything but creative. With a strong foundation for how math is used and its potential for solving problems, young children can get the right start to their relationship with math. Children can build solid foundations (and have fun) through models and concrete experience.

Math Models

As with all areas of creativity, the best way to introduce and encourage mathematical thinking is to uncover opportunities for your child to see math everyday. Point out mathematical thinking just as you would a work of art or a beautiful song. Talk to people about the different ways they use math. You will soon find that math is everywhere: incorporated into sports, medicine, writing, maps, weather, art, philosophy, religion, astronomy, games, architecture, and most any other discipline you can think up.

Of course, the most influential models for a child are her parents and caregivers, so be sure to point out the way *you* use math in everyday life. Some examples might be:

- Sewing or handwork: counting stitches, using patterns, calculating size
- Shopping: working within a budget, calculating price per pound, using scales, making price comparisons
- Paying bills: organization of materials, using and balancing a checkbook
- Cooking: measuring, doubling or halving a recipe, using fractions, dividing food items among guests
- Gardening: measuring width between rows or seed sowing depth, dividing a plot, building a perimeter fence, measuring temperature, recognizing seasonal change and passage of time, counting seeds, dividing the harvest
- Building: How wide should the sandbox be? How many materials do we need?
- Household duties: sorting toys and laundry, making and measuring out cleaning supplies, sending mail, arranging furniture
- Planning: using calendar and time skills
- At your job, if you work outside the home

Provide opportunities for everyday math to occur in concrete ways other than paper and pencil and straight computations. Children spend too much time learning calculations through pencil and paper methods. When children from the United States have been compared with their international counterparts, it is the ability to thoughtfully solve real-world problems where they come up short. Children who are exposed to mathematical thinking early in concrete and tangible ways are more likely to be able to grasp concepts later.

If you are bringing your own struggles with math to parenting, it will be especially important to provide concrete experiences and ways of mathematical thinking to life for your children. At the same time, it will offer you a way to reconnect with math in a different way and stimulate your own creative thought. It does not need to be a solo journey. As you begin your mathematical journey, do it together and make it magical.

HOW TO SOLVE A PROBLEM

Solving problems is at the heart of building creativity. Having the skills to solve a problem is perhaps the most important element when embarking on your creative mathematical journey. Instead of telling children how to solve a problem, ask questions. Help them find their own methods for solving the problem. Some methods for problem solving that will evolve for a young child include:

Act it Out

Young children often need to use their bodies or other types of manipulative items (beans, coins, blocks, and the *handiest* ones—fingers) to solve problems. They have not yet internalized enough background knowledge about numbers and number combinations to mentally perform math problems (although some may be able) so provide opportunities for children to act out problems with their bodies or material objects.

Draw a Picture

Many young children enjoy drawing. If you have a problem you are trying to solve, let them draw to find the answer. "We have three cats, two dogs, and one fish. How many animals do we have in all?" Use drawn pictures to make maps of their bedroom, your house, yard, or garden. Let your child experiment with rearranging the furniture by using small pictures of each item on a larger piece.

Guess

Estimation is an art, and like all other forms of art, it takes practice. If you can incorporate estimation into your life, this will be foundational to your child internalizing guessing and estimating into their problem solving repertoire. Estimate everything from how many steps it will take you to get to the car to how many toy dinosaurs will fit in the measuring cup. When children have a good idea what an answer might be, they are able to measure their results against it. The more estimating you do, the better children become at using the skill to solve problems.

Make it Simple

When we ask children to do math, we oftentimes are asking a lot. If your child is trying to solve a problem that feels difficult, help her break it down to a simpler problem, maybe even a simple problem she has already had practice with.

Look for a Pattern

Seeing patterns is foundational to being a good mathematician and developing an understanding for how numbers work together. Without it, you have only your memory to rely on in math. When your child is trying to figure out how many forks and spoons to bring to the breakfast table, guide him in counting by twos.

MATH TOOLS

The foundation of any math learning comes from exploration with materials, finding patterns, and exploring with combinations and groupings. Exploration of math materials, like using blocks to explore symmetry or dividing up the cookies in an equal way, allows for more creative thinking and problem solving. At the same time, it incorporates play into real world concepts and simulations.

Having the tools children need to explore math is as important to their creative growth as anything. In order to become a mathematical thinker, a child needs to have opportunities to experiment and explore concrete materials before being expected to move onto abstract thinking. With a variety of math tools available to them, children can begin to gain experience with mathematical concepts. With basic experience, they can then begin to question, analyze, make their own problems, and tell about their discoveries. Through this they will be on their way to becoming creative thinkers who view math as a useful tool.

Counting Tools

A common starting place for young children is counting. Opportunities for becoming familiar with number sequence are ever-present in the life of children. They count their family members, the steps up to their room, and how old they are. Daily counting and the repetition that counting brings provides a foundation for other math concepts such as measurement, computation, and patterning. Beans, cubes, coins, forks, spoons, stones, shells, nuts, fruit, Legos™, blocks, small animals or dinosaurs, and popsicle sticks are all wonderful counting tools. In addition to providing sufficient experience counting in numerical order by ones, also count backwards, and by twos, fives, and tens.

Number Tools

Once you have given plenty of opportunity for making collections and counting, provide occasion to see numbers in various ways. When developing your print environment, use numerical numbers as well as the number words. Through the use of a family calendar or family news (see Chapter 20, *Words My Way*), you can

"Not everything that counts can be counted, and not every-thing that can be counted counts."

Sign hanging in Einstein's office at Princeton

point out places you see numbers being used in everyday life such as house numbers, on stamps, the clock, speed limit signs, on money, in coupons, and at the grocery store.

Introduce the use of dots, either on dice or dominoes, and tallying to count. With experience using varying number forms such as dot counting, children begin to make the pattern connections in their head and will learn to identify the numbers by their placement on the die (i.e. two groups of two make four). This will be foundational to other forms of computation such as addition, multiplication, and division as children grow.

Pattern Tools

Patterns are the foundation of math and number combinations. Providing opportunity to scc and cxperience patterns is as important as giving opportunities to count and explore numbers.

Almost anything can be a pattern tool. Many young children enjoy using pattern blocks, which are small, geometrically shaped, colored plastic or wooden pieces. Use a mirror to explore with patterns you are making with your blocks. Tape two small mirrors together and explore with what happens to the objects placed in front of them. What happens if the mirrors are at 45 degree angles? 60 degree angles? 90 degree angles? Use skewers to serve food in patterns. When you are writing a story together, write one word in red, the next word in blue, the next word in red and so on. Look for patterns in your everyday world: on the road, at the store, on your clothes, in artwork, and at the park.

Children will begin their pattern exploration with simple patterns such as black, white, black, white, black, white. As you are looking at and creating your own patterns, challenge children to make a more complicated pattern. "Can you add a third color?" "What happens if you do black, black, white? Can you repeat that?"

Make Your Own Geoboard

What You'll Need:

One 12-inch square piece of pressboard or other soft wood
100 small nails
Hammer
Measuring tape or ruler
Pencil
Colored or plain rubber bands

Directions:

1. Measure one inch down and one inch from the left edge of your board. Mark the point with your pencil. Repeat this on the right edge.

2. Place your ruler on the board and align your two points.

3. Mark every inch. You should have ten points across your board.

4. Hammer a nail about 1/3 of the way down into each point.

5. Measure one inch down from each nail to make another line of points and nails.

6. Repeat this until you have ten rows of ten nails.

7. Use your rubber bands to make triangles, squares, pentagons, hexagons, octagons, and other shapes and patterns.

Patterns are all around us, and the more you look for them, the more you find! The more you find them, the more you can incorporate them into your math explorations. The more children incorporate them, the more they will develop deeper understanding of patterns and mathematical thinking.

Sorting Tools

Children learn the valuable mathematical skills of sorting, classifying, matching, and organizing when they are involved in everyday tasks such as putting toys away, helping with laundry, sorting and organizing their books by author or subject, and unloading the dishwasher. In playrooms, provide low shelves and individual bins for small toys, so children can easily see where all of the different objects belong. Label them for an added language experience: trucks, trains, blocks, games, mammals, dinosaurs, stamps, paper, or clay tools. See Chapter 3, *Breaking Ground*, for more information about setting up and organizing your environment.

Other items that are fun to practice sorting might include: mixed beans, a collection of buttons or beads, or natural materials found on family walks. As you sort objects, talk about the properties of each. You might find several different ways to sort the same objects. You might sort by color, shape, texture, or size.

Calculation Tools

Fundamental to mathematical thinking is calculation, which is simply the combining of numbers and objects. But calculation does not need to begin and end with pencil and paper. For children to internalize number combinations and groupings, they need to experience computation and calculation in real life situations. With a *real* problem to solve, the experience takes on *real* meaning.

Provide opportunities for children to combine in many different ways. Uses abacuses, beads, or other manipulative items you have collected for counting. Guide children in making combinations of these items by asking questions such as "How many more shells would you need to have ten?" "There are six of us, and we have three sandwiches. What should we do?" Or "I have two forks here. Can you bring enough so we have five?"

For further exploration into computation, introduce calculators. Let children use them for simulation play in their restaurants, post offices, and grocery stores. Begin by just allowing exploration.

Measurement Tools

Children of all sizes enjoy measuring experiences. The best place to start with measurement is with non-standard measurements (feet, forearms, and other items that change depending on whose body you are using) and move to standard measurements (paper clips, cubes, coins, rulers, yard and meter sticks, and tape measure).

Introduce scales, rulers, protractors, balances, temperature gauges, and even string to help children learn to measure in different ways. Use gallon jugs and other plastic pouring containers and measuring cups to measure water in the bathtub. Involve children in daily cooking measurements. See Chapter 13, *Thinking Outside the Recipe,* for ideas about cooking with children. Through experimentation with different types of measurement materials, children will gain practical lessons in volume, capacity, and fractions.

Measuring time is also a way for children to develop necessary math understanding. Stock up on clocks of all kinds and stopwatches. If you are buying a toy clock for your child to practice making different times, consider a sturdy Judy® clock (available at teacher supply stores) which has gears and accurately simulates the positioning of the hands on a real clock. Incorporate calendars that show the whole month and calendars that show just a week at a time into your home. Keep a monthly calendar of your family activities for your child to refer to. Talk about days of the week, yesterday, today, and tomorrow. Talk about how the sun and the length of the shadows it produces have been used to measure the day. The moon can be used to measure a month.

Be sure at some point to introduce and speak about metric measurement. While it is not standard in the United States to measure using metrics, it is widely used in the sciences and around the world.

Geometry Tools

When children experiment with geometry and use geometry tools, they refine their problem solving skills. Using geometry tools usually requires planning, deductive reasoning, critical thinking, and discovery. The best geometry tools for a child are blocks of all shapes and sizes. Through block play, a child learns about shape, line, patterns, width, height, measurement, perimeter, area, classification, symmetry, equality, inequality, and mapping. In addition to maple blocks, introduce pattern blocks or make your own using colored paper for alternative block play experience. Geoboards, square wooden or plastic boards with spaced pegs for attaching rubber bands, are also a wonderful way for children to make their

Computer Programs that Explore Mathematical Thinking

Anno's Learning Games (Putnam New Media, ages 6-10)

Countdown (Voyager, ages 5-12)

James Discovers Math (Broderbund, ages 3-6)

Math WorkShop (Broderbund, ages 5-12)

Microworlds Jr. (LCSI, ages 3-7)

Millie's Math House (Edmark, ages 2-6)

Money Town (Davidson, ages 5-8)

PuttPutt (Humungous, ages 2-8)

Snootz Math Trek (Theatrix Interactive, ages 5-9)

Thinkin' Things (Edmark, ages 2-8)

Where's Waldo? At the Circus (WarnerActive, ages 4-9)

own shapes, designs, and geometric patterns. They are available at teacher supply stores or you could make your own (see sidebar on page 170).

However you experiment with geometry, be sure to also point out shapes in everyday life. "This park is a pentagon." "Look at that diamond on the road!" Or "that building is symmetrical. If I could fold it in half it would be exactly the same on both sides."

MATHEMATICAL VOCABULARY

As you begin to explore math tools and concepts with your children, always be mindful of using math vocabulary when talking about your own thinking and how you solve a problem.

If children have opportunities to hear and familiarize themselves with math words being used in their everyday life, the concepts will not seem so daunting to them. Some simple (but important) math vocabulary you might use include:

Number Words: ordinal numbers (first, second, third)

Time Words: afternoon, calendar, clocks, evening, morning, seasons

Direction Words: above, after, before, below, between, bottom, inside, last, left, next, outside, over, right, under

Computation Words: add, minus, plus, subtract, take away

Comparison Words: alike, equals, equal parts, halves, heavier, less, lighter, longer, longest, more, middle, not alike, same, sort, shorter, taller, tallest

Geometry Words: circle, cone, cube, cylinder, pattern, rectangle, shapes, square, sphere

Money Words: dime, dollar, nickel, penny, quarter

Measurement Words: length, long, height, short, tall, wide, weight, width

As you are going through your day, model mathematical thinking by using these and other math words. "Let's see. There are sixteen people coming to your party. 2, 4, 6, 8, 10, 12, 14, 16. I have enough napkins." Or model addition strategies by counting up and adding using your fingers: "I have 5, and I am adding 3 more. Five. . . six, seven, eight. So five and three added together equal eight." The more you talk about your own mathematical thinking, the more your children will start to do the same and develop strategies for solving problems.

Explore the magic math has to offer. As you journey through mathematical thinking together, you'll begin to see creativity and problem solving emerge.

Picture Books Involving Creative Math Themes

Number and Counting

A Grain of Rice by Helena C. Pittman

How Many Snails? by Paul Giganti, Jr.

How Much is a Million? by David M. Schwartz

Mouse Count by Ellen Stoll Walsh

One Hundred Hungry Ants by Elinor J. Pinczes

Ten Apples Up on Top by Theodore Le Seig

Ten Sly Piranhas by William Wise

Computation

The Doorbell Rang by Pat Hutchins

Eating Fractions by Bruce McMillan

Measurement

As the Crow Flies: A First Book of Maps by Gail Hartman

How Big is a Foot? by Rolf Myllar

Inch by Inch by Leo Lionni

Ten Beads Tall by Michael Twinn

The Very Hungry Caterpillar by Eric Carle

Time and Money

Bennie's Pennies by Pat Brisson

Chicken Soup with Rice by Maurice Sendak

Clocks and More Clocks by Pat Hutchins

The Grouchy Ladybug by Eric Carle

Geometry

Block City by Robert Louis Stevenson

Bridges by Ken Robbins

Castle by David Macaulay

Grandfather Tang's Story by Ann Tompert

The Shapes Game by Paul Rogers

Shapes, Shapes, Shapes by Tana Hoban

Spaces, Shapes and Sizes by Jane J. Srivastava

The Village of Round and Square Houses by Ann Grifalconi

Classification, Collections, and Sorting

Anthony Ant's Treasure Hunt by Lorna and Graham Philpot

Aunt Ippy's Museum of Junk by Rodney A. Greenblat

The Button Box by Margarette S. Reid

Caps for Sale by Esphyr Slobodkina

Everybody Needs a Rock by Byrd Baylor

The *I Spy* series of books by Walter Wick and Jean Marzollo

If You Look Around You by Fulvio Testa

On My Beach there are Many Pebbles by Leo Lionni

The Yellow Button by Anne Mazer

chapter 18

Lightbulb Moments

Science to Foster Creativity

Children wonder. Each day they reach out in new ways, ask questions, and ultimately try to make sense of the world. It has often been said that the child is an intuitive scientist. Some controversy has arisen over this metaphor in the scientific community, largely in part because up until recently, we have had little information about the way scientists approach problems, think, and reason. We often hear about scientists having a sudden flash of insight. Researchers studying the creativity of scientists see it as following the same mental processes guiding other forms of creativity. Poets, artists, musicians, and scientists all follow similar paths leading to their discoveries. While there are many instances of spontaneous discovery, it is in the slow incremental building of theories that children play out the role of the scientist.

THE CHILD SCIENTIST

We know that scientists build theories. They wonder about ideas and make multiple attempts at testing those ideas. Sometimes they confirm their thinking. Sometimes their ideas are found to be wrong and with new results their thinking is changed. This process, known as the scientific method, also mirrors the way a child moves through each day.

From birth, children are careful observers of the world. As they grow and become toddlers, they begin to add increased communication to their repertoire to further make sense of the world. They talk, laugh, ask questions, and begin to express their ideas in other ways such as drawing pictures.

Children, like scientists, are also avid sorters and classifiers. They take the information they gather through their "research," which in the case of young children is simply living, and put it into categories that make order and sense of the world. From this process, they make predictions. "If I let go of this spaghetti, will it fall on the floor?"

Before their fifth birthday, children can develop an understanding of complex causal relations in many scientific areas including physics, biology, and psychology. But they will only be able to do so by being given true opportunities for experimentation. That goes beyond following simple directions and working through a rigidly planned experiment. Instead, it means having access to the materials and ideas and having guidance in designing their own experiments. It means discovering through trial and error. And it means not getting it right the first, second, or third time and trying again.

Happy Accidents and Careful Observations

Science is often inspired by mistakes and the careful observation of nature. It has been said that paper was first discovered by observing wasp nests. Tea is believed to have been first made in 2373 B.C.E. when Chinese Emperor Shen Nuy was boiling water and leaves fell into his pot and began to brew. Peanut brittle was accidentally made when a New England woman added baking soda instead of cream of tartar to her taffy. Chocolate chip cookies were first made when a baker added her chocolate too late in her process and it didn't have time to melt. Velcro was inspired by the sticky burrs that remained after a walk in the woods.

While all these examples are often referred to as *happy accidents*, they also require someone to think creatively and carefully observe those everyday instances. Since children are such careful observers of the world, they are ripe with possibility for growth in scientific thinking.

Science is Everything

What is science? The word *science* comes from the Latin word *scientia*, which means to know. For this reason, science has been largely defined as a body of study and knowledge. However, science is also the experience and the act of finding answers, or simply finding more questions. A good science experience for a child is one that encourages the search for questions and answers, allows for creativity, and promotes problem solving.

It's no secret that science gets *taught* on certain days and irregularly in schools. In the home, science is all around. Part of nurturing a creative spirit certainly means setting up ways children can test ideas, make mistakes, and change their thinking through science. If scientific thinking, intrinsically interesting materials, and good questions (see Chapter 4, *The Art of Questioning*) are present in the home, then science is bound to happen more often; children will be poised to think more scientifically and more creatively.

SCIENCE TOOLS

Having the tools that encourage discovery and scientific thinking will support your child as an intuitive learner and creative scientist. Like all tools, if children have access to them easily and regularly, they will be more likely to use them spontaneously. They will develop a comfort level with the tools and use them for a variety of purposes.

Science tools can seem endless. Provide a variety of them for children to first explore with and then use purposefully. Like other supplies used for creative development, make sure you introduce them slowly so they are not overwhelming for your child.

Containers

As young children explore the world, it is valuable for them to have access to interesting objects to explore with. Fill containers large and small with interesting media such as water, oatmeal, rice, dry beans, or pebbles. Provide small containers to scoop up the materials, and experiment with capacity. Use containers to collect things found during outdoor explorations or to sort and classify. Don't forget to collect rainfall!

Collections

Allow for exploration and experimentation with collections of recycled items or other groupings of items such as paper clips, rubber bands, marbles, rocks, gems, or small mirrors. Collect natural items found on your walks such as shells, stones, leaves, bugs, sticks, pinecones, and moss. Keep jars or tubs of magnetic and non-magnetic items (paper clips, washers, erasers, feathers, beans, coins, magnets, etc.) for your child to experiment with. Collections of items like Geomags and a little imagination go a very long way. Of course, be sure to keep small objects and choking hazards out of the reach of infants and toddlers.

Magnifiers

Stock your science area with different types of magnifiers. Try hand-held magnifying glasses of all sizes and the collector types that allow for a child to place an insect or other nature finds inside. Don't forget a nice set of binoculars and a microscope. Consider also investing in a digiscope, which (for about one hundred fifty dollars) allows you to connect your microscopic finds to your computer. Beware of binoculars and microscopes labeled age-appropriate, as they are often cheap imitations with not much power and may not have the ability to excite your young scientist in the same way as a decently powered one could.

The Great Outdoors

There is no greater science lab than the great outdoors. However large or small, outdoor spaces can lead to wondrous discoveries. Provide opportunities for exploration on the sidewalk, in open meadows, on wooded trails, around ponds, near oceans, and other bodies of water, if you can.

Being outdoors allows for many up close observations of life cycles. Know that a butterfly net doesn't just collect butterflies. Swipe a large net in any long grass and you'll like be able to observe all kinds of amazing creatures. When exploring the great outdoors, make sure you do it at different times of the day. Try

"To myself I seem to have been only like a boy playing on the seashore, and diverting myself in now and then finding a smoother pebble or a prettier shell than ordinary, whiled the great ocean of truth lay all undiscovered before me."
—Isaac Newton

Wonder Words

your hand at sundials. Experience lunar cycles, eclipses, constellations, nebulae, meteor showers, and other wonders of astronomy.

Recording Devices

As.children grow in their scientific thinking, they will likely want to record their findings. Use tape recorders to take verbal notes or record sounds. Take photos or video clips. Use a notebook to write down ideas or draw pictures of your observations.

Access

When your children have questions or are wondering about something, it is essential to have access to the tools that will help them enrich their questions or find answers. Access to the Internet can be extremely valuable to the young scientist. Use it to watch Quicktime videos of young cheetahs playing or astronauts in space. Use email to contact professional scientists and university professors; they are very willing to talk to kids wanting to know more about what they do and have been known to provide tours of labs, speak to groups, or even take on young "apprentices."

Finally, read, read, read! Read about scientists. Read picture books about animals, weather, geology, fossils, and other explorations into the wonders of nature. Read non-fiction books that explain the forces of nature. Read scientific journals and interesting newspaper articles with your kids. Read the weather page together.

Household Tools

Common household items (flour, salt, sugar, food coloring, cornstarch, baking soda, vinegar, oatmeal, corn meal, etc.) have many uses for the child scientist. Explore with oil and water, baking soda and vinegar. Keep food coloring on hand as it is an amazing collaborator with milk and cream. Additionally, food coloring is essential to add to oceans in a bottle, volcanoes, and homemade flubber and oobleck. See Chapter 12, *Splish! Splat! Smoosh!*, for fun, messy recipes.

Random household items, the kind that live in your junk drawer or otherwise haven't found their rightful home, make wonderful science table items for exploring texture and buoyancy properties. Try an extra piece of Velcro, the old piece of corrugated cardboard, random pieces of Tupperware, feathers, straws, zippers, string, or material scraps. Keep cleaned eye droppers from medicine bottles and measuring spoons for your scientific explorations. Add some goggles to protect the eyes.

Light Tools

Light carries energy and is wonderful to play with, bend, split, and join. Use prisms and mirrors to experiment with light. Use the sun and leaves or random household items to make your own sun prints on colored construction paper, explore with sundials, and learn about shadows. Keep a full powered flashlight and mini flashlights to explore with light; peek under rocks and in caves.

SCIENCE TOGETHER

The image of the lone scientist is a vivid one for many people. However, research on how scientists think and reason suggests scientists find working in groups more effective. Ideas are generally formulated by working off the ideas of others. Scientists who work together use different kinds of strategies to explore many different questions, explanations, and causes which helps them to overcome bias in their research. As Isaac Newton suggested, we work better and more effectively when we are "standing on the shoulders of giants."

The home is ripe with opportunities to explore science together. You only need to look inside your cupboards to find the tools with which to do so. Explore, experiment, question, observe, and be creative! Science is one of the best tools to get you there.

Resources

Fiction Science Books to Explore Together

Diary of a Worm by Doreen Cronin

Diary of a Spider by Doreen Cronin

If You are a Hunter of Fossils by Byrd Baylor

Millions to Measure by David Schwartz

Non-fiction Science Books

Caves: Mysteries Beneath Our Feet by David Harrison

Hurricane Tornado published by Dorling Kindersley

The Best Book of Fossils, Rocks, and Minerals by Chris
 Pellant

Eyewitness Books such as *Crystal & Gem* and *Rocks &
 Minerals*

Greater Explorations in Math and Science by Lawrence Hall
 of Science (otherwise known as GEMS) units such as:
 *Animal Defenses, Build It! Festival, Bubble-ology,
 Terrarium Habitats, Tree Homes, Of Cabbages and
 Chemistry,* and *Oobleck: What Scientists Do*

Let's Go Rock Collecting by Roma Gans

Life on Earth: The Story of Evolution by Steve Jenkins

Scholastic Discovery Books such as *Light, Weather,* and
 Water

*Science in Seconds for Kids: Over 100 Experiments You Can
 Do in Ten Minutes or Less* by Jean Potter

*Secrets of Sound: Studying the Calls and Songs of Whales,
 Elephants, and Birds* by April Pulley Sayre

Maryland's Geology by Martin Schmidt

The Visual Dictionary of the Earth published by Dorling Kindersley

Volcanoes: Journey to the Crater's Edge by Philippe Bourseiller

What Makes a Magnet? by Franklyn Branle

Whirligigs & Weathervanes by David Schoonmaker

Who Eats What? Food Chains and Food Webs by Patricia Lauber

chapter 19

tell me a story

Using Storytelling to Enhance Creativity

Once upon a time a very special adult planted a seed, a seed called magic. This magic was in the form of words, spoken with a special quality of voice, and a thrilling look in the eyes. Each time the words were uttered and the eyes opened, a heart was uplifted and a spirit born. They all began with this…"Tell me a story!"

Storytelling is among the most exceptional activities we can engage in with our children. "So many adult-child activities require the adult to reach down to the child's level or the child to reach up to the adult's," said librarian and storyteller Jeff Defty. "Storytelling is a unique meeting ground, a place of shared meaning where no one has to pretend they're interested in something beneath or beyond their years. It is a place where we all get to be merely human."

In this chapter, we will explore the many ways storytelling benefits children, the elements of creative storytelling, and how to incorporate this art into your daily lives.

WHAT STORYTELLING PROVIDES

Telling stories aloud is different than reading stories. It requires a whole new listening skill set and stimulates the brain differently than reading. It uniquely provides many opportunities for connection with each other, creative development, and simply our humanness. Among the many benefits of sharing our own personal stories are the following:

Intimacy

Telling stories is great fun! They can get us laughing and bring us closer together. Perhaps there is no better reason to tell stories than to spend time doing something fun and snuggly with our children, families, and friends.

Passing on Stories

Give your kids the precious gift of the past with a few good hand-me-down tales. Storytelling offers a way for our children to discover history, other cultures, or simply learn about what Grandma did as a little girl.

Becoming Literate

Storytelling offers our kids extended development of vocabulary, listening skills, and story structure. It is another wonderful tool along their journey to becoming literate.

For Future Use

Yes, telling stories can actually build a foundation for the future. Just as we might turn to books to handle a difficult situation in our children's lives, perhaps the telling of stories can even do more since it is coming from a trusted adult source, in their own words. Retelling fables and sharing morals gives children a foundation for future use. Similarly, parents can share stories about a time they went to the hospital, moved houses, lost a pet, or learned something new.

Creativity

Storytelling has its obvious and not-so-obvious advantages, but a wonderful reason to tell stories is that they build creativity and imagination. Once a child's focus is on the actual decoding of the words on the page, the *experience* changes for them. While some of us may be excited and passionate about our children being able to read and decode at early ages, there are other considerations to our enthusiasm. The continued use of storytelling in the home will enrich a child's thinking, imagination, and the reading process.

THE ART OF STORYTELLING

Telling stories can feel awfully daunting. Once you have a few storytelling tricks under your belt, the process will get easier and the creativity will emerge.

Memorable Moments and What You Know

Start here. Tell what you know. Tell what you remember. Any memorable moment will work. For some time in our house, "Ouchy Stories" have been a huge hit. From the iron that fell and left the scar gracing Dad's arm to the biking accident that left Mom with a permanent bruise under her left eye, any detailed memory about a time when one of us got hurt is gold in our house. Tell about firsts or funny happenings that involved your child or someone they love. The day a child was born or adopted is often a hit.

Innovate

Take a story you know well and make it different. Change the setting, change key props, or change the ending. A good place to start is fairy tales or other folklore (see resources at the end of this chapter). Using predictable stories like Joy Cowley's *Mrs. Wishy-Washy* (who often becomes Mr. Squishy-Squashy) is another source for easy creative stories. You can retell any familiar story and change the little details (like what the character was wearing or eating to meet your child's likes and dislikes) or change the ending to make it less scary, more inclusive, or funny.

Learn Key Phrases

Many memorable stories have key phrases that are all a parent needs to remember when telling a story. So use those commonly known phrases such as "Run, run as fast as you can" and "My what big _____ you have" to make your stories connect with your child's already growing knowledge about the world. Stories can go on and on and take all kind of exciting turns when you know a few simple key phrases. We still haven't found an item that won't fit into the beloved "Brown bear, brown bear, What do you see? Well, golly gee, I see a stop sign looking at me!" Certainly a nice alternative to "I Spy" when you are driving down the road and feel in need of a quick story.

Practice

When I first started telling stories, I was admittedly horrific at it. So much so that I have actually been known to stop in the middle and change the activity because I was so embarrassed at the turn the story had taken. Still, I forced myself to keep trying and have now become someone who can whip out a story at a moment's notice. What I have come to realize about my own stories is that my five year-old listener is laughing because he finds it genuinely funny. He is truly enjoying the experience, and appreciating that I am making a fool of myself, which is often the case.

Eyes on the Prize

Don't forget to keep good eye contact with your *audience* when telling stories. It will help them stay focused and know that you care about this special time together. Your eyes will be very useful in conveying the meaning and feeling of your story. Roll them, bat them, flutter them, keep them wide open and intense, or hide them momentarily.

Use Your Own Words

Don't worry about trying to recite your child's favorite story word for word. Remember, your story will change every time you tell it. Children will likely correct you on some of the important details now and again, but make the story your own by using your own words. In order to personalize the story more, add your child's name, friends' names, pets, grandparents, cousins, and places you enjoy like your favorite park or restaurant.

Audience Participation

Never underestimate the power of audience participation. As you are going through a story, stop for just a moment to give some thinking time. Little pauses in the storyline will likely be filled in by even your youngest listeners. Making a story a joint venture also takes a huge weight off your story-bearing shoulders and will usually make the story more interesting and take unexpected turns. Allow your child to decide who the characters will be, where the story takes place, what the conflict is, and eventually how it all gets solved. This way, a story turns into a two player game where you both win.

Include Modalities

For some children, listening to stories for any length of time can be difficult if their learning styles are not catered to. Consider adding other props to help make the story come alive as well as tapping into your child's own learning style. Use shakers, puppets, a piece of string, a flashlight and your hands, drums, a favorite teddy bear, or a special rock. We often tell stories, even retell stories, using our piano where emotion, tension, or sheer delight can easily be conveyed. Use sound, sight, smell, and touch. Change your voice, make a funny facial expression and use movements like running in place or squashing through the thick mud to help tell the story. The possibilities are endless. See Chapter 3, *Breaking Ground*, for more information about learning styles, modalities, and Multiple Intelligences.

Read, Read, Read

The more you read and learn the structure of what makes a story exciting to your children, the more stories will begin to emerge in your household. Retell what you read. Tell new stories about some of your favorite characters. Maybe even make up stories about some of your favorite authors.

WHAT TO TELL: THE STORY TREASURE TROVE

Folktales

If you are not at all versed in them, there are many versions of every kind of "how the (fill in the blank) got its (fill in the blank)" stories. Make up your own or use ones you have read.

Here are a few favorites:

Aesop's Fables retold by Leo Lionni

Anansi the Spider: A Tale from the Ashanti by Gerald McDermott

Arrow to the Sun: A Pueblo Indian Tale by Gerald McDermott

Baby Leopard: An African Folktale by Linda Goss

Baby Rattlesnake by Te Ata

The Fairy Tale Treasury by Virginia Haviland

Jabuti the Tortoise: A Trickster Tale from the Amazon by Gerald McDermott

Little Rooster's Diamond Button by Margaret Read MacDonald

Raven: A Trickster Tale from the Pacific Northwest by Gerald McDermott

Papagayo: The Mischief Maker by Gerald McDermott

Peace Tales: World Folktales to Talk About by Margaret Read MacDonald

Stories to Solve: Folktales to Talk Aloud by George Shannon

Traveling to Tondo: A Tale of the Nkundo of Zaire by Verna Aardema

Zomo the Rabbit: A Trickster Tale from West Africa by Gerald McDermott

Wordless Picture Books

Another great way to start is with wordless picture books. Never underestimate the greatness of a wordless picture book. They are often overlooked by parents seeking to provide literary experiences for their beginning readers, but wordless picture books are often the best model for story structure (beginning, middle, end). They offer a wonderful opportunity for children to play with language as they tell their own versions of what the characters are thinking and saying. Here are a few great wordless (or almost wordless) picture books that will require you to use (or hone) some of those storytelling skills.

The Grey Lady and the Strawberry Snatcher by Molly Bang

Little Star by Antonin Louchard

The Mysteries of Harris Burdick by Chris Van Allsburg

The Red Book by Barbara Lehman

Sidewalk Circus by Paul R. Fleischman

The Snowman by Raymond Briggs

Tuesday by David Weiss

Guided Imagery

A great way to help your child use her imagination fully is to guide her through some imagery. With eyes open or closed (usually the easiest way to see the picture in the mind) lead your child through some images such as a leaf falling off a tree, the balloon that got away, the salmon in the stream, a squirrel preparing for winter. Don't forget to add cues that will help your child imagine all their senses being used during the journey. See Chapter 15, *Jump, Jiggle, Jive*, and Chapter 16, *Music in Me, Me, Mee!*, for more about using guided imagery with music and movement.

Family Folklore & Myths

These are the best kind of stories. From Grandpa's story about the cat who slipped down the chimney to the dinosaur that took a bite out of mom's favorite hat, family folklore is magically delightful. When I was little, a common story my dad (who otherwise wasn't a big storyteller beyond "This Little Piggy") told was a family myth about how the windshield wipers worked. Who knew that there was actually a bird in there that would spit on the window when you pressed that little button?

Childhood Songs

Songs and poems can have great stories in them. From old favorites like *The Eensy Weensy Spider* and *Wheels on the Bus* to your own family favorites, use them to make new stories. Find a song or poem of which you like the cadence. Retell it as is or spice it up with some new words to your old tune. It could be as simple as singing *Animals on the Train* instead of *Wheels on the Bus*. Or you could take it a sillier direction. In our house, this usually looks something like the "Name Game" where only the first letter is changed and the words become new nonsense words.

Ghost Stories

It seems that some children never tire of the intriguing aspect of scary stories. If it is appropriate for your family to tell scary stories, a great place to start is the simple old tale *In a Dark, Dark Wood*. It is easily innovated upon to meet the characteristics of your own living space, and many kids love playing with their voice and then loudly yelling "Boo!" at the end. Add a flashlight to the scene for an extra special tale time. If your children are extra sensitive about scary stories, the message can be something we thought was scary turns out to just be a shadow or the squirrel tapping on the window asking for more nuts to add to his winter stash.

Here are a few resources for other scary stories to tell:

Scary Stories to Tell in the Dark: Collected from Folklore by Alvin Schwartz

More Scary Stories to Tell in the Dark by Alvin Schwartz

The Thing at the Foot of the Bed and Other Scary Tales by Maria Leach

MOMENTS IN STORYTELLING TIME

Storytelling is something that can be squeezed in at almost any time during the day or night. Be sure to take advantage of:

Car Rides

Especially long car rides can be hard on our little ones. But even the short ones can sometimes get monotonous. We tend to listen to books on tape when the rides get long, but have really enjoyed our own storytelling time as well. We once planned a ten-hour trip in the middle of the night in order to maximize the sleep factor for our son. Lo and behold, he was wide awake at 2 a.m. What could have been treacherous turned out to be a fabulous early morning of telling a very involved and creative story about a monkey who went from star to star as we drove along, incorporating everything we passed on our journey.

Waiting

Fill those times when you are at the bus stop, in the doctor's office, or on the front porch waiting for a friend, with a story. Use the setting of where you are waiting to experiment with your stories.

Meals

A great time to share stories is at the dinner or breakfast table, especially if the whole family is involved. Do a shared story where each family member provides a detail or tell individual stories.

Bedtime

There's perhaps nothing more enchanting than laying in the dark with your eyes closed telling tales as they pop into your mind. To make this an ever-special ritual, take the same character on a series of adventures night after night and you'll soon have traveled around the world.

Active Time

Use stories to help focus and channel your child's active energy. Tell the story *Where the Wild Things Are* and they can pretend to be Wild Rumpus-ing. And what little one wouldn't want to attempt spinning in the *Red Shoes*? Together, try making up a story and let your child act it out, which may require darting from one end of the house to the other several times. What fun! What better way to spend those active moments?

Groups

Sometimes when you get a few families or groups of children together, it can get a little hectic. In times like that, try storytelling to focus them all together. Try playing a story game where each person adds a unique piece to the story and then passes to the next person.

Bad Days

I actually like to refer to them as days that offer a lesson, but nonetheless, they may also be described as just plain bad days. If you are a human being and parent, I'm sure I don't need to tell you about them. So after one of these trying days, spend time winding down together with a story that has nothing to do with the day you just had. It will serve to reconnect you with each other. If you dare, perhaps your story can be about what happened in the day. Who knows, the disaster might just end up sounding a bit funny. You might end your bad day laughing.

Enjoy those special magic storytelling moments, however they uniquely manifest themselves in your home!

Other Resources for Storytelling

There are some wonderful books that will get your creative storytelling juices flowing.

Hidden Stories in Plants: Unusual and Easy to Tell Stories from Around the World Together with Creative Things to Do While Telling Them by Anne Pellowsi

HomeSpun: Tales from America's Favorite Storytellers by Jimmy Neil Smith

Juba This and Juba That by Virginia Tashjian

Keepers of the Earth: Native American Stories and Environmental Activities for Children by Michael J. Caduto

Personal Journaling by Donald Davis

Tell Me Another: Storytelling and Reading Aloud at Home, at School, and in the Community by Bob Barton

chapter 20

Words My Way

Creative Writing for the Young Child

Like sunrises over distant seas, writing begins early and then continues with each new day. But unlike the sun, we need to nurture it for it to keep returning and shining on.

Regardless of whether or not they have been on elaborate or fancy vacations or how many toys have come into their households, children have a wealth of experiences to draw upon to practice writing. Writing about what is important to your child as a form of personal expression is a valuable undertaking.

In this chapter, you will find many ideas for exploring creative writing in your home. As children begin to write, keep in mind that it is important for them to try their own spellings and be allowed to use them regularly. Children moving through the development of writing will begin by drawing "scribbles," lines, or other symbols to represent letters and words. This kind of writing is all very purposeful and valuable for the development and future enjoyment of writing. As prewriting children gain experience with writing, their words will begin to incorporate initial letters and other prominent sounds they hear in a word, which will include ending letters and eventually middle consonants. With experience in playing with language, using words, and writing them purposefully, the mechanics of writing will emerge. For young children, if writing focuses on conventions such as spelling, capital letters, and punctuation, the danger is that we will create children who just do not enjoy writing. The importance of writing for creativity's sake should never be underestimated.

EXPRESS YOURSELF

In Else Homelund Minarik's famous book *Little Bear's Friend*, Mother Bear asserts, "Little Bear will soon be going to school. There he will learn to write." While a precious story for many reasons, the reality is if parents wait until their children become school-aged for them to experience prewriting activities, they will have missed out on very important building blocks in the creative process.

Prewriting Activities

Prewriting activities serve to get children used to the movements their hands will make when they write and strengthen the muscles in their hands in order to develop their fine motor skills. Actions like cutting lines—straight lines, curvy lines, spirals—or cutting out shapes, works muscles in the hands needed for the physical act of writing. Likewise, using clay or kneading bread dough are great opportunities for getting ready for the act of writing, as will painting, drawing pictures, and using stencils. As children begin to recognize letters, they can also learn to form them. Start with a sensory experience and write letters, shapes, or numbers in salt, mud, or goop.

Besides the actual coordination of being able to physically form letters, children need to hear writing, whether in the form of oral stories being passed down (see Chapter 19, *Tell Me a Story*), or books being read to them. Without this background in story, children will not want to or be able to move to the next stage.

Word Games

Writing begins orally. Play these word games to stimulate the creative use of words in your home:

- Word Association. One player begins by saying a word. The next player says the first word they think of. For example, I say "monkey" and you say "jungle." Then I say, "trees" and you say "grow." The game continues on for as long as you can come up with associations.

- Rhyme. Begin with a word of your child's choosing. Volley back and forth trying to come up with rhyming words.

- Silly Sentences. Use a long or funny word to create silly sentences. "Elephant" is usually the word of choice in our house, but the word "ouch" gets frequently used as well.

- Give Directions. Make a cake, pizza, or even sushi together aloud. Each person decides what will be added next as a topping but needs to also remember the previous toppings in order. Try to add the silliest toppings you can think of.

- Word Train. Make a word train by starting with one word and then using the last letter or sound to begin a new word. For example, I say "monkey" and you say "yarn." I say "nose" and you say "elephant."

- Words Within Words. As children begin recognizing and reading small words such as to, in, and by, they will also notice them inside other words. For older children, try to make as many small words as you can out of a longer word.

Signs and Labels

Reading and writing do not happen in isolation. Provide a print-rich environment, one in which children see words regularly even before they begin to read them independently. Signs have been a favorite of children and a fabulous way to get children to begin writing. One mother of two young boys has a running rule that after a certain time in the evening, the "kitchen is closed." Her boys were often asking, "Is the kitchen open yet?" They found it exciting and novel to make an open and closed sign for Mom to turn over when the kitchen entered each stage in the day. Make labels for household items or your own open and closed signs for specific rooms. But don't stop there. Signs can be unique part of your child's creative play. As children engage in different types of play, such as simulations, encourage them to add signs to their make-believe restaurants, banks, train stations, and lemonade stands. Consider also labeling items such as refrigerator, door, chair, and other items around your home.

Oh Lovely Lists!

Lists often permeate the lives of adults. In busy lives, we need them to function in a world of to-do's. Since this may be one of the many writing experiences that children see their parents engage in regularly, that makes it one of the best kinds of writing for them to emulate. Children can make their own to-do lists, a sort of daily plan for themselves. This is a great morning activity or even a great way to start off the week. "Play with Sam, brush teeth, clean my room, tell Rufus a story before he goes to bed." For extra support, provide a list of commonly used words, such as colors, numbers, names of friends and family members, days of the week, and common activities, and display them in a prominent place or near to where your children will spend time writing. As your children come across new, exciting, or interesting words while you are reading, add them to these lists for future use in their own writing.

Tickets

As children engage in other simulations, such as running a theatre, puppet show, a theme park, carnival, circus, or zoo attraction, they will likely find opportunities for writing through making tickets. Together, make blank tickets for easy access and encouragement.

Yummy, Yummy Recipes

Recipes are a wonderful writing opportunity for children. Make a personal favorites recipe book or have your child tell you the recipe they have created or what they think goes into their favorite soup or sandwich. The writing of a recipe gets children ready to think about the importance of steps in writing and making sure the correct sequencing and details are there. If you forget to write down that the cookies need to be put in the oven, they won't turn out.

"What makes for great art is the courage to speak and write and paint what you know and care about."

—Audrey Flack

Letters

Letters and notes are simply wonderful ways to communicate and express our thoughts and voices. In fact, letter writing is a fabulous way for children to develop their writing voice. As well, it can offer a special way to connect with relatives and friends. Write out the invitations to a sing-along or other celebration or gathering. Write letters to favorite authors or characters. Send them care of the publisher. Make it a field trip to see how the post office works—they give tours—and then write about your trip! Send postcards to friends, even if they only live next door.

While it is valuable for children to have plenty of practice in forming letters and putting those letters together to make words, it is equally useful for them to use computers as a means of writing and communication. Emailing family and friends and composing letters and stories on the computer is perhaps one of the best ways to encourage creativity on the machine that has permeated our twenty-first century lives. My son and his friends often sent each other emails with seemingly random-typed letters. In their prewriting stage, the letters were representations; what looked random to us adults was very clear in the minds of these four year-olds: "Please come to the pumpkin patch with me," or "Thanks for being my best friend," they would tell us. Being able to write stories and letters in this way is an important practice in developing a clear voice and practice in creating written pieces. As well, it gives ownership to their writing processes.

Family News

Family newsletters do not just need to happen during the holidays. They can be a way to write and communicate with each other all year long. So often in our busy lives we need to find rituals in which we report to each other what is going on in our individual lives. Consider setting up a news center in your home

words my way 199

where each person can add the happenings in their own lives. This activity brings families with many children, especially ones that have children of widely varying ages, together and allows for further connection while practicing writing skills. Families can tell stories this way too. One person writes a beginning and each family member adds to the story over time.

Logs

Keeping different types of logs can help spark creative ideas and stories. Try keeping reading logs of stories you have read and enjoyed, recipe logs, logs of what you did during the week, logs of favorite music and lyrics to your favorite songs, or a log of all the stories you have written.

Stories

Telling and writing stories are often the most obvious forms of writing and can also be the hardest for people to do. When your children are just learning to write, take dictation. Write statements and stories exactly how they say them. Stories can be unique made-up stories or a reporting of actual happenings with a twist.

Guide your child in writing comics to go with your child's illustrations. Write about a trip you went on. Stories can be as little as one page or several pages long. Don't be afraid to just write a simple story now and then. Every work doesn't need to turn into a novel.

Keep a collection of all the stories told in your family typed up on the computer and kept as a family anthology. For ideas about what and how to tell stories, see Chapter 19, *Tell Me a Story*.

Research Projects

Reading and writing about non-fiction subjects are often a favorite among children, especially as they grow into school-age. Research, the act of discovering more about a subject you are interested in, is a wonderful way to keep children questioning and learning.

Talk to your children about what research is. Begin incorporating the word into what you are already doing. When you find a banana slug making its way through your garden and your child asks why it has all that slime, you can say, "Let's research that!"

Once you have a question or topic, the research methods will begin to emerge. Introduce your children to research using books, magazines, and newspapers. Use the Internet, photos, movies, and personal interviews. You can research informally or take a more formal approach. Once you have gathered your information, organize it, and, if you desire, publish your findings. Consider making posters, news reports, or a recording of the report.

Poetry

Poetry is anything and everything you want to write, speak, scream, sing, or whisper! So when you are discovering and writing free verse poetry with your kids, the rules are, there are no rules! As you begin your poetry adventures, go on a poem scavenger hunt. Find poems that make you feel happy, sad, silly, or quiet inside. Find poems that rhyme and ones that don't. Find poems written by a variety of poets. Explore the work of Emily Dickenson, Jack Prelutsky, Langston Hughes, Shel Silverstein, Judith Viorst, Cynthia Rylant, and Eve Merriam. Read poems that are written in different forms: free verse, haiku, acrostic, shape poems, and nonsense.

Keep in mind that poems are not just found in poetry books. Sometimes the best poems are found in children's picture books; the medium of illustrated children's literature lends itself so well to great poetry. See the end of this chapter for a list of a few wonderful picture books that are in poetry form. There are many, many others so please don't limit yourself to just these.

As you discover a variety of poetry, read them aloud. Read them outside, inside, at the dinner table, with listener's eyes closed, and any other ways that might help the poem come alive in your child's head. Read the poems with a normal voice, then over again using different expressions or becoming the character.

Once your children have had ample opportunity to experience other people's poetry, they will likely begin speaking or writing their own. Keep a notebook designated for family poems and record your child's poetry when the inspiration hits. These poems could be lists of words, lyrical stories, information about an animal they have learned about, alliteration of sounds they hear, nonsensical combinations of words, or words to live by.

Good Writers...

- write everyday
- daydream
- write different things (books or stories, newspaper articles, songs, poems)
- tell stories
- keep a writer's notebook and journals
- make changes to their writing to make it better
- use good word choice
- "grab" their readers
- evaluate their writing
- illustrate
- write about their experiences

THE PROCESS

Besides providing all these wonderful ways for children to express themselves through the written word, there are other considerations as we begin the process. As mentioned previously, the process of writing begins long before a child has the motor ability to put pencil to paper and scrawl out his or her own words. Very young children enjoy stories in general and especially enjoy reading the same ones over and over again. This can even be more so when they are sharing their own writings.

Examples

The greatest spark for a child wanting to write creatively is if they see other people in their lives do it with regularity. Share what you have written, either past stories or projects. However small, take time regularly (perhaps as a ritual each day) to share something you have written: a list, a note on the calendar, a poem, a song, a short story, or ideas for the future Great American Novel. No idea or piece you share is too little or too big for a young writer in need of a model.

Brainstorming Ideas

After reading a variety of different types of writing, by many different writers (which many children have done by a very early age), it is time to come up with some ideas for our own writing. Even your young child can keep a list of stories she wants to tell. Make a brainstorming ideas list to help spark new ideas. Keep it in a special place for when you get stuck for ideas.

Delicious Words

Delicious words are the kind of words that are so good and so wonderful, you just want to eat them up. When you are writing, think about ways you can say something with "delicious" words (ones that appeal to their senses) instead of words like "good," "bad," "pretty," "cute," or "soft." Help your reader to feel, taste, and smell your writing by using words that can help them make a picture in your mind. Keep a "delicious words" list hanging somewhere in your house and add to it often.

Writing Time and Space

Write with your children in different places often. Visit parks, rivers, lay under trees, the bathroom, kitchen, or a favorite cozy closet. Try going to new places to write to help get the family's creative juices flowing. While it is important to have new experiences in writing, it is also especially valuable to start a routine in your family's writing. Some writers and poets find it very valuable to write in a special place as soon as they get up in the morning (often called "morning pages") to help with creativity. A few minutes of *same place* writing in addition to the *different places* writing will add dimension to your writing. If you so desire, set a writing time where the whole family can write the family news, stories, poems, songs, or draw pictures.

Sharing

Even though writing is something that can be as private as you want it to be, try to find the pieces that you feel like sharing. Have a Poetry Celebration or a Writer's Café. Invite your family. Eat cake. Serve sparkling cider. Do a reading of everyone's writing and bask in the glory of being a writer.

Because all writers are different, there is no one magic answer that will work for everyone. Our job, as parents and learning facilitators is to relax! Providing ample and varied opportunities and modeling writing will help us to find the answer that will work for our creative kids. The number one point to remember is that you are not on a schedule. Go out and dig in the dirt and try it again before dinner, after dinner, after a bath, curled up in front of the fireplace, or lying under the oak tree. Provide the support system that every writer needs, because you don't want writing to be a struggle.

Expressing thought through written language is a celebration!

Do. . .

- Allow your learners to choose what will be written and when writing will happen.

- Read aloud everyday!

- Draw pictures.

- Play with words. Make up silly, nonsense words. Have fun with it.

- Share ideas together.

- Model behaviors of a good writer!

- Talk about what makes a writer. Make your own list about what good writers do.

- Keep a writer's notebook. Having a special place where you are putting your thoughts down will make all the difference in the world.

- Go to author signings and readings.

- Conference. Take time to talk about what you like about a particular piece of writing and what you are still wondering about.

- Share.

- Allow the use of invented spelling. It is more important to get ideas down than to have words spelled correctly. The conventions will come with experience. Confidence, comfort, and ownership of the writing process must come first.

- Encourage conventional spellings by keeping lists of commonly used words: days of the week, family members' names, number words, color words, or other words your child wants to spell.

- Celebrate your child's writing through parties, writing groups, and readings.

- Laugh.

- Offer suggestions, but say "I'm wondering about..." instead of "That part when such and such happened doesn't make sense."

- Take dictation (even from older children).

- Keep reading and writing logs.

- Have fun and enjoy the experience!

Don't. . .

- Make writing happen at a certain time.

- Make writing a punishment, i.e. writing a letter of apology (unless it comes from them and they choose to say sorry in that way, etc.)

- Make your child "publish" everything.

- Criticize spelling or grammatical errors (it will certainly inhibit the creative process!).

Writing Resources

Picture Books and Videos About Writing

The Alphabet Tree by Leo Lionni

Arthur and the Poetry Contest by Stephen Krensky

Arthur Writes a Story A Video about Marc Brown

A Cake for Herbie by Petra Mathers

Emily by Michael Bedard

Joy Cowley Writes by Joy Cowley

"The List" and "The Letter" in *Frog and Toad* books by Arnold Lobel

Love that Dog by Sharon Creech

Long is a Dragon: Chinese Writing for Children by Peggy Goldstein

Once Upon a Cool Motorcycle Dude by Kevin O'Malley

Wise Old Owl's Halloween Adventure by Robert Kraus

Some Great Picture Books that Use Poetry as Text

Charlie Parker Played Be Bop by Chris Raschka

Life Doesn't Frighten Me by Maya Angelou

Have You Seen Trees? by Joanne Oppenheim

Have You Seen Bugs? by Joanne Oppenheim

I Live in Music by Ntozake Shange

In the Small, Small Pond by Denise Fleming

In the Tall, Tall Grass by Denise Fleming

Mud by Mary Lynn Ray

My Mama Had a Dancing Heart by Libba Gray Moore

Rain Talk by Mary Serfozo

Red Rubber Boot Day by Mary Lyn Ray

Time for Bed by Mem Fox

Wild Child by Lynn Plourde

Other Writing Resources

Boy Writers: Reclaiming Their Voices by Ralph Fletcher

Calligraphy for Kids by Eleanor Winters

Games for Writing: Playful Ways to Help Your Child Learn to Write by Peggy Kaye

Growing Up Writing: Sharing With Your Children the Joys of Good Writing by Linda Lamme

The Poetry Break: An Annotated Anthology with Ideas for Introducing Children to Poetry by Caroline Feller Bauer

What a Writer Needs by Ralph Fletcher

chapter 21

Media iN MotioN

Using (and Not Using) Media to Develop Creativity

"You can't control the waves, but you can learn to surf."
—Sri Swami Satchidananda

Media is a tricky issue. The Internet, computers, film, radio, television, and advertising are a pervasive and ambivalent presence in our lives. They are a collective force that could be said to be the best and worst thing that has ever happened to us. Wading through the research about the effects of media on children is not always helpful. Research can sometimes seem inconclusive and often contradictory regarding whether media, despite having some educational value, is healthy for young children. One thing we know for sure is that media can be and is regularly used as a creativity tool, and many people express themselves through it. In this chapter, we will explore the ways in which we can engage present media tools to deepen creativity. Through this kind of engagement with media at a young age, we take a step towards nurturing critical thinkers who are able to negotiate these evolving technologies as adults.

TV OR NOT TV? THAT IS THE QUESTION

By the age of five, the average American child will have spent more time watching television than she will have spent speaking with her father her entire life. By the time he enters first grade, the average American child will have watched the equivalent numbers of hours to receive a four-year college degree. These hours will have been spent just *watching*, at a time in their lives when their brains are growing faster than they ever will again, and patterns are being determined and set.

Over the course of any given year, the average American child spends 2,400 hours in front of television. That's 2,400 hours less time telling stories, dressing up, taking walks, finding and making treasures, and testing their own theories about how things work.

As reports of this abundance of television watching suggest, parents are choosing against the America Association of Pediatrics (AAP) recommendation that a child under the age of two years have zero hours of television watching per day. While many parents feel that watching TV didn't have negative effects on them as children, what is not to be underestimated is the increasing targeting of children as television advertising becomes more savvy in its attempt to get children to buy things and become brand loyal from this very early age.

While many parents will continue to keep their television dial turned to the ON position, it is important to find the balance in how and when it is used. Many parents report that once they come to agreement about using less television, amazing creative ventures begin to emerge in their children. They play more outside. They read more and their play becomes more imaginative. So, for creativity's sake, it is worthwhile to reconsider the amount or use at all of television in the lives of young children.

MEDIA MULTITASKING

More and more bedrooms are becoming media centers where children have the television on while working on a computer. From a very early age, as young as six months in some cases, children are developing a relationship with media like never before. The AAP recommends pediatricians "encourage parents to make thoughtful media choices and limit children's media exposure to one to two hours per day." Even that seems like too much media when you consider that a child is only awake for approximately ten to fourteen hours a day, with many of them spending a significant amount of that time in school (where media is also often present).

Develop Limits Together

Dictating to children what they can and cannot do does not contribute to the development of a creative, thinking, conscious spirit. Explain your concerns about media in an honest, non-threatening way. Come up with a time that sounds reasonable for the family to view and use media together. Make a schedule. Keep a media log or diary that tracks how much media each family member is regularly using. Include television, computer use, and video games. Come up with a list of other activities to engage in instead and post it somewhere in your home as a reference. Whatever limits you come up with, develop them together. Once you do, you can then be free to further look at the content of the media by deconstructing it.

Deconstruct Media

Swimming in the sea of media, two situations often happen. We either don't see all the messages our brains are trying to process, or the messages feel so strong it is as though we are on the verge of drowning. Parents can help children rediscover themselves in the vast sea by helping bring awareness to the messages that are being sent, breaking them down and analyzing them together. With the media you come in contact with, deconstruct it, take it apart and view it critically, together. While shopping, point out product placement and fancy packaging. When coming in contact with ads on television, billboards, other forms of print media or the radio, engage in conversation about who paid for it, what the advertisers are trying to get you to buy and why, and what strategies they are using, such as celebrities or appealing to certain emotions.

MAKE MEDIA A CREATIVE FAMILY MATTER

So what is a parent to do? While media has powerful potential to create apathy and dependence, it can also serve as an opportunity to enrich thought processes, personal expression, and ultimately be a point of connection. Fortunately, the ways in which families can take personal control of media are plentiful.

Make Your Own Films

The art of motion pictures offers many opportunities for children to develop creativity. Film is a medium in which we can witness wide varieties and examples of creativity. After reading a book together, use movies as follow up to a book or unit of study. Talk about choices the filmmakers made. What was left out? What was different? How were they similar? What were some of the creative aspects of the film? Costumes? Music? Lighting? Animation?

Then, rather than just be an audience member, tell your own family stories through filmmaking. Even young children will enjoy the view from behind the camera and the editing process. If you are working on a Macintosh computer, iMovie is a simple program that even young children can navigate and use to create something extraordinary. Consider using stop animation with clay figures children make themselves or setting up puppets and toys. Add voice to the story, and voilà! Children can easily make their own film and tell their own story. Film can also be used to record children's scientific findings, art projects, or even as a medium for a family news segment. Through the experience of making visual stories, children can become more aware that every story they see is also made; the images become less sacred as your child develops a more critical eye.

Computers

Computer software is certainly rich with potential for creative development. Unfortunately, it means wading through many "drill and kill" type programs in order to uncover the gems. Unless you are doing that wading late at night or in the wee hours of the morning when the children are asleep, it is done at the expense of the children. As we look at programs that encourage children to create and imagine, keep in mind that a *good* piece of software is one that allows children to use it in many different ways and offers opportunity for them to follow their own interests.

There are a few especially good programs that develop creative thinking and problem solving and that provide open-ended options to encourage children to use divergent thinking:

Logo Programming

Microworlds by LCSI over the years has offered the best in programming for children. Microworlds, which used to be geared towards older children and was the precursor to Lego™ robotics programming, has become especially user friendly for even young children. Along with other programs such as *My Make Believe Castle*, a demo program of *Microworlds Jr.*, for ages 3-7, is available for downloading at http://www.microworlds.com/.

Scratch

This wonderful program offers kids an opportunity to create multimedia projects online by snapping together graphical blocks. The intended age is 8 and up, but it seems user friendly enough for young children to use with support. At least for now, the creators at MIT Media Lab are offering this as a free download at http://scratch.mit.edu.

Kid Pix

If you can get your hands on an earlier version of Kid Pix, consider it a gold mine. The newer versions have all the fancy bells and whistles we have come to expect from media these days, which could be a bit distracting. Still, whether you use a new or old version, Kid Pix provides a good medium for creations through drawing, painting, stamping, adding sound and simple animation.

Kidspiration

Similar to Kid Pix, Kidspiration allows young children to record stories, make pictures, and add sound. This is an especially good program for young children to report their scientific findings, create presentations of their writing, and practice certain math skills such as sorting, categorizing, and making diagrams.

Math Programs

See the resources at the end of Chapter 17, *Everyday Math Magic*, for a listing of math software that requires critical thinking and problem solving.

Wordprocessing

A child's computer use need not be flashy software. Write stories using the word processing software you already have available. Simple typing can help a child create and develop ideas through keyboard play that begins with instant silly, nonsensical words and eventually becomes a simple tool for children to record wonderings about the world, questions they have, and poems or songs they write. With word processing programs, children and families can create simple newspapers, signs and labels, and write letters to friends.

Web Pages

Web development is increasingly becoming an exciting way for children to express themselves and share their lives with people around the world. The ability to make a web page is more accessible than ever to young children. Through programs such as Dreamweaver, children can add their own text, pictures, and sounds to create a web page. But don't think you need a special program to do it. Within most word processing programs you can take any document and convert it to html, the format for a web page. Beyond that, increasingly sites such as easysite.com offer quick, easy, free webpage development, but it is recommended that children not use identifying information such as phone numbers, addresses, and last names on webspaces such as these.

Internet

The Internet offers a multitude of fun and content area learning. For well-monitored kid-friendly research online choose sites like kidsclick.org, thinkquest.org, or askforkids.com which all provide ad- and popculture-free web searches for children. Many games, puzzles, and mazes can be found for free and plentifully on the Internet. Here's a few that provide a creative, problem solving experience:

Curiosoft: http://www.curiosoft.com

Kids Domain: http://www.kidsdomain.com

KidPsych: http://www.kidspsych.org

Discovery: http://www.school.discovery.com/brainboosters/

Enchanted Learning: http://www.enchantedlearning.com

Digital Cameras

Digital cameras have entered our lives with great force. While it is often the parents who are looking through the lens, photography is a wonderful way for children to experience media and be creative. Digital cameras for children are getting better (and cheaper) all the time. They provide an easier way for children to experiment with photography by easily being able to delete pictures they don't think "turned out." Use your photos to make a scrapbook or collage, or add them to your web page.

Radio

Use radio as an example for another way media is used. Listen to radio shows to get a feel for how music and commentary are woven together. Record your own stories, songs, and your family's original musical composition. Make your own radio show for news issues that are important to your family. The New Mexico Media Literacy Project suggests deconstructing media by making counter ads (i.e., an ad for an imaginary toy). Perhaps your children want to make an ad expressing the wonders of playing in the woods. Consider visiting a radio station to see how it all works behind the scenes.

Books about Media

Amusing Ourselves to Death by Neil Postman

Four Arguments for the Elimination of Television by Jerry Mander

Parenting Well in a Media Age: Keeping Our Kids Human by Gloria DeGaetano and Diane Dreher

Screen Smarts: A Family Guide to Media Literacy by Gloria DeGaetano and Kathleen Bander

FINDING BALANCE

Media is something we cannot ignore. It is all around us. It is part of our everyday lives. For better or worse, we are a society saturated in it. In the twenty-first century, we use media in almost all areas of our lives so we do need to bring awareness to how that may effect our children. With a balance of its use and a critical eye, the negative aspects of media can be avoided. As media researcher Robert Sylwester finds, "Children who mature in a secure home/school with parents/teachers who explore all of the dimensions of humanity in a non-hurried accepting atmosphere can probably handle most electronic media without damaging their dual memory and response systems."

Newspapers, computers, movies, television, billboards, radio, magazines, and Internet: with awareness, effort, and practice, we can learn to use them to our advantage for the further development of creativity and a child's critical engagement with the world.

Internet Resources

Cable Access Centers (Community TV):
    http://www.bevcam.org/peg/alpha.htm

The Center for a New American Dream:
    http://www.newdream.org

National Alliance for Media Arts & Culture:
    http://www.namac.org

National Federation of Community Broadcasters (Community
    Radio): http://www.nfcb.org

National Institute on Media and the Family:
    http://www.mediafamily.org

New Mexico Media Literacy Project:
    http://www.nmmlp.org

Media Awareness Network:
    http://www.media-awareness.ca/eng/

PBS Youth Media Network:
    http://www.pbs.org/merrow/listenup/links/youthmedia.html

Worldwide Network of Students Making Movies:
    http://www.makeamovie.net

part 4

THE ONGOING JOURNEY

Celebrating the Creative Spirit

let's paint this place lipstick red
and dancing

chapter 22

the other side of the mountain

Celebrating Creativity

A master who lived as a hermit on a mountain was asked by a monk, "What is the Way?"

"What a fine mountain this is," the master said in reply.

"I am not asking you about the mountain, but about the Way."

"So long as you cannot go beyond the mountain, my son, you cannot reach the Way," replied the master.

For many children, from a very early age, the gold star and the "good job" is the mountain that prevents them from finding their Way. Once they enter the school systems, as most children do, the stars get bigger and brighter and the *Way* seems even cloudier. When giving praise or positive reinforcement, there is certainly a fine line between encouragement and evaluation. With too many "good jobs" lathered on children, we take the risk of them losing their intrinsic pleasure in the act. Children should be able to think, wonder, learn, and explore without having to worry about how good they are at any given skill, or if the adults around them think it is worthwhile. So celebrating creativity is not about giving praise or rewards based on achievement. Nor is it about bribery or incentives for kids to express their creativity. While these may work on the short term, in the long run praise and rewards have been found to damage a child's sense of worth, confidence, and internal drive. Celebrating creativity is about truly exulting what gives joy to each individual child.

CELEBRATING CREATIVITY

Celebrating the activities your children have shown interest in, not just been successful in, is about spending quality time with children and experiencing the activities they love just because it gives them joy. It is not just a way to say "I'm proud of you!" or to add a gold star to a chart. It extends far beyond that. Without evaluating performance, celebrations of a child's expressions encourage present and future pursuits and give confidence in and courage to try to new things. These are vital ingredients in building the creative spirit.

WAYS TO CELEBRATE TOGETHER

Celebrating creativity is an exploration into a child's passions. When children move away from needing praise for something they have accomplished, celebrations start to look a bit different and are less about external motivation, if at all. The ways in which you celebrate will be as varied and unique as the children in your lives.

Host an Opening

Host a gallery opening and display your child's artwork, Lego™ creations, sculpture, sewing, or knitting. The celebrant can give a "lecture" about her style and what she has learned.

Have a Ball

Host a game of soccer or whatever sport your child enjoys. Invite family and friends and play a game together in your celebrant's honor.

Reenact

If your child has been reading books of a certain genre, time period, or author, hold a book party and dress up like characters or stage a reenactment. Serve refreshments.

Be Jammin'

Hold recitals or jam sessions for any child learning to dance or play an instrument or for one who just likes to explore in music making. Even if your child is only taking a bow and has yet to learn any particular piece, a small recital or get-together with other aspiring musicians can be wonder-filled on many levels!

Hit the Road

Host a hike in your child's honor to celebrate interest in nature or to learn more about your local forestry service. Bike to a nearby nature preserve or museum and stop for ice cream along the way.

Read All About It

Hold a book fair. Get together with your friends and share the books, poems, or songs you have written. Wear sunglasses and snap your fingers!

Eat Your Heart Out

Go out to breakfast. This can be a particular treat if you or your children are often involved in morning activities that prevent you from spending that special pre-day time together. Take a midweek jaunt to your child's favorite restaurant or let your child choose dinner and *go with the flow* even if that means you are eating pancakes with watermelon and french fries.

Yes Days

Hold a Yes Day. Do whatever your child wants to all day long. Go on his schedule and leave when he is ready. See Chapter 6, *Yes Days,* for tips about planning and holding a Yes Day.

Honor Each Other

Hold a family Honoring Day. Have each family member prepare something special. Share appreciations and favorite moments with each other. Perhaps prepare a slide show with pictures of all the fun you have had together. You can treat it formally, with official ceremony, or informally, with the conversation held around the dinner table or other special meeting place.

Communicate

Write poems or letters back and forth with each other. Even your pre and early readers and writers will love communicating about things they learn and what is exciting about their lives. See Chapter 20, *Words My Way,* for more about writing letters and poems together.

Whether your child wants to have a special one-on-one dinner or be surrounded with friends and family, let her choose how and with whom she would like to celebrate something she loves doing. As the focus turns away from the *good job* and more towards the exploration and celebration of joy, you will be well on your way to the other side of the mountain.

chapter 23

MY treasure House

Displaying Creativity

"Open your own treasure house and use those treasures."
—Zen Koan

Displaying the many varied ways children express themselves provides a child with an opportunity to revisit the process of creating, reflect on that process, and share the product with others. Regardless of the product, there are just as many ways to share as there are to create.

CREATIVITY ON DISPLAY

Wall of Fame

Find a place in your home where you can create an Art Wall, Gallery, or Wall of Fame, and display your children's work. This might mean a stairwell, hallway, or even the front window. If you use the front window as your display area, you instantly double your space because work can be facing in and out.

Rotate

If space is tight for displaying works of art and other pieces of creative expression, try having a special fancy frame, usually found inexpensively at garage sales or second hand stores, to rotate work through. Try a large gilded frame for that museum look! A screen saver with your child's work will also do the trick.

Perfectly Portfolio

Portfolios, a collection of a child's work, show growth over time, are generated by, and empower the child. They are truly authentic, show a variety of work, and provide real life learning opportunities. See article insert, *Tips for Creating a Portfolio*, for more information.

Hanging Around

Use clips (either in a designated art space or your child's room), wire, or string to hang works of art from the ceiling. Add them to a coat hanger for a more portable hanging device.

Local Opportunities

Most communities have opportunities for children to display work. Sometimes you just have to look for it. Many local libraries offer some of their display cases for children's collections or work. City Halls are often happy to let you use their wall space or bulletin boards. Even local gift shops or other places of business are happy to display work created by local children. Radio stations may even allow an extra bit of music-making live on the air. You only have to ask.

MAKE A MUSEUM

Children now have many opportunities to gain experience in visiting museums. You most likely have gotten to know your local art, natural history, and science museums well. Now's your chance to take it even further. Make your own!

Creating museums, galleries, and living history (depictions of the past, reenactments, time period replications) instills pride and accomplishment and gives ownership to one's learning. In the process of gathering materials, setting up exhibits, and explaining concepts in a way that others will be able to comprehend, children cement their understanding.

Tips for Creating a Portfolio

Discuss

Discuss as a family: What is a portfolio? Who uses them? Why? Get in contact with some working artists, architects, etc., and ask them to share their portfolios with you. Discuss how portfolios create a great keepsake, holding your treasures for years.

Set Goals

The key to using a portfolio system in your learning environment is for your learner to become self-reflective, to get to the point where she is evaluating her own work critically, compassionately, and for her own improvement. And the first step to getting to that point is to set goals together as a family. Write them down. Include dates. Reevaluate, and set new goals when necessary.

Keep a work folder from which you can make selections from once a month or once per season. A portfolio is NOT a work folder, but rather selected pieces that show growth over time, which leads to the next point.

Show Growth

Compare items such as writing samples side by side in order to show growth in spelling, handwriting, vocabulary, voice, ideas, organization, content, and word choice.

Choose a Medium

Choose a medium and size that works for your family. Portfolios can take many different shapes. They can be in the form of photo album-like folders, large homemade books, interactive CDs, websites, and the list goes on. They can have pockets, fold out pages, pop-ups, or anything else that makes them come alive.

Be Consistent

Use a layout that one can follow easily. That can be anything from a theme throughout the portfolio such as *A Day in the Life* to just using the same type of dividers or color-coding for readability.

Choosing Work

Allow children to make the majority of the selections. Remember, this is the learner's portfolio, not the parents'. She may not always choose pieces that you think are the *best* or show the most growth. That may be a difficult thing to stomach. The value will come in her identifying what she is most proud of, rather than what others deem as *good*. As a parent, perhaps you want to keep your own scrapbook so you make sure to save all *your* favorites.

Reflect

Sprinkle choices with written descriptions of the projects and/or reflections on attitude towards the work. Parent and child can individually or together write a description of the task presented or skill being worked on with regards to a few particular pieces. This is where your opinions can come in. Offer to write up a parent reflection for how a specific activity went.

Organize

Choose an organization method. Portfolios can be organized in many different ways. Decide as a family (or let you learner decide) how the portfolio will be organized—by subject, chronologically, etc. Add a Table of Contents and an Index: A reader of a portfolio (just like a book) should always be able to know the contents and where to find each subject. Creating a Table of Contents or Index is a valuable organizational tool. If the child does not yet know how to use one, it will surely be a good lesson.

How Often?

Choose pieces often enough to be sure that you are comparing work from the same time period.

What to Include

Include personal favorites, reports, photos, newspaper clippings highlighting the learner, volunteer experiences, journals, drawings, experiments, explanations, checklists, rubrics, self-evaluations, and self and parent or mentor comments.

Be a Model

Start working on your own portfolio for what it is that you are learning, be it art, writing, teaching, website design, documenting a special hobby, or a project at work. Do it together.

Share Your Portfolios

Share with each other, with family members, and with your friendship group. Have a Portfolio Party! Make and send invitations. Celebrate your successes and look forward to future successes together!

Natural History Museum

If you are one who collects fossils or has other nature interests and collections, set up your own Natural History Museum. Get your other geologist or paleontological friends to join you and make it a neighborhood Natural History Museum.

Science Museums

Set up science experiments that cover the topics you have studied. This could be like a science fair, but try to make it more an exploratory discovery museum for young and old. Consider having themes such as inventors, machines, or other exhibits that require thinking.

Museum Websites

Fine Art Museums of San Francisco:
http://www.thinker.org

National Gallery of Art Kids Homepage:
http://www.nga.gov/kids/

The Metropolitan Museum of Art—Explore and Learn:
http://www.metmuseum.org/explore/index.asp

Museum of Modern Art Safari—An Adventure in Looking:
http://www.moma.org/momalearning/artsafari/index.html

Smithsonian for Kids:
http://www.si.edu/kids/

Living History Museum

Let the kids search around in the attic to find the things you used as a kid and let them go to town. Introduce them to items like: one old piece of silverware that has a story to you, eight-track tapes or old 45 records, the manual typewriter, the pre-transistor radio, old costume jewelry, books, magazine clippings, toys from Grandma's childhood, birth announcements, classic games like jacks or jump rope, or an old version of Monopoly, bobby pins, curlers, an old phone, and the list goes on.

Art Gallery

Display your works and have a reception. Serve goodies and give a lecture on your style. You may even consider having a small auction and donating the money to your favorite charity. Once you have decided to set up your gallery or museum, think about having an opening, running an exhibit for a period of time, opening it up to family, neighbors, or even your entire community.

All Aglow in the Work

As children become more and more interested in sharing their experiences with others, they often develop a cache of their creations and a desire to experience entrepreneurship.

Kid-run businesses can easily be turned into the museum gift shop. Allow children to set up shop with greeting cards or candles they have made. Let them include some of their handmade items: musical instruments, origami creations, or sculptures. Don't forget to include a few homemade cookies or muffins; every museum needs a snack bar!

Happy displaying and appreciating together!

Dare to Dream: Goal Setting Tips

Just as we may set goals for ourselves, guiding our children in goal setting is valuable to their own creative development. Studies show that children (and adults) who define their own goals and reflect on their struggles and accomplishments, are more likely to have success with what they are trying to achieve.

Goal setting is an important link in the family chain that binds us all together. Through mindful self-reflection and daring to dream together, creativity and the family partnership towards it will grow in its own unique and creative way.

Mindful Self-Reflection

Mindful self-reflection, a crucial step in goal setting, is the place of calm we don't necessarily will ourselves to be in but rather find ourselves in when we are truly ready for a creative leap. Being able to reflect mindfully is to enter a place of calm clear thought so that ideas can flow through us, and we are then able to pull a few out for our use. Teaching mindful self-reflection to children takes patience and good modeling. We want our children to hold onto their spontaneity and creative energy, and one way they can do that is to have plenty of moments of calm and quiet, and ultimately self-reflection.

Dare to Dream

Many people who advocate goal setting insist that a goal must be realistic. While the sentiment is valid, we must also realize that goals in the mind of a child will not always sound realistic, but are actually very possible with imagination and creativity. So when your child says that she wants to ride a unicorn over the rainbow so she can dance with the Giggle Fairy in Lompa Land, take it seriously and embrace it as a part of her goals. It is only by encouraging thinking VERY BIG that we will raise the creators and thinkers of the world.

Monitor Progress

As your family begins to breathe life into your stated goals, you might often find yourselves straying from project to project or new ideas might be spurned by the original plan. In our family, one of the many reasons we like to write them down is so that we can bring our focus back when needed. For children and adults alike, every two months is a good interval in which to reevaluate goals. If that feels like too often, try sitting down with your goals at the change of seasons.

Model

Like any other aspect of creativity, the more we model ourselves in the act of reflection, goal setting, and evaluation of our own progress, the more likely our children will give it importance. In our house, goal setting takes on many forms: simple daily goals and plans made at the start of each day, to a monthly calendar of activities, to even larger project boards that show goals we want to accomplish within a season or the whole year. But modeling goal setting means even more than that.

Children need to see the adults in their lives both setting goals AND working to attain them. For me, this has meant consciously changing my routine. I used to try hard to get all my exercise and writing in before the household awoke so my energies could be focused on them. That meant getting up very early, which was fine and even enjoyable. What I realized though was that some of my most important goals and their processes were never being witnessed by my family. So while I don't want to write an entire novel in the presence of my child, he now knows what I am working towards and gets to witness the hard work involved in my own varied personal projects. It even means that he willingly joins in my yoga practice and sits down to write alongside me. It's an added bonus when we get to create together.

So think of yourself as a facilitator of wonder. Reflect mindfully. Define your goals together. Model. Most of all, dare to dream!

Resources for Making Museums and Kid Businesses

Better Than a Lemonade Stand: Small Business Ideas for Kids by Daryl Berstein

Kid Biz: Year Round Money-making Projects for Young Entrepreneurs by Bonnie Drew

The Kids' Natural History Book: Making Dinos, Fossils, Mammoths & More! by Judy Press

Off the Wall Museum Guides for Kids by Ruthie Knapp

chapter 24

reach for the moon, catch the stars

Appreciating Our Creations

If you shoot for the moon, you will land among the stars. What better place to be? Sparkling, twinkling, and spreading light for a very long time and a very long way.

We are born to attend to a journey, a journey of seeking, a journey that is absolutely original and absolutely unique for each who follows his own path. Just as each journey is unique so will be the properties and characteristics of each journey. Creative expression will look different for each individual. In this way, creativity doesn't always manifest itself the way we would imagine or even maybe the way we would like. It takes its own turns and unfolds in ways we could never have imagined.

ACCEPT THE PROCESS

We don't teach children to walk. But we do find ourselves coaching them as they move through their process—pushing themselves up, scooting or crawling along in their own way, eventually cruising along the furniture. Finally, they are standing on their own to take the first wobbly steps that lead to the days where they are full force running. Once that happens, we often forget what it was like to not have a walker. Any fears we once had that walking wouldn't happen on a certain timeline disappear, for the process proved itself to be as natural as taking a breath. Creativity, catching the stars as we are up there reaching for the moon, is just as natural, if we can allow it to be.

The process of catching a star is not an easy one. Oliver Jeffers, in his picture book *How to Catch a Star*, whimsically illustrates the process. A young stargazer loves stars and wants to catch one for himself. His process is creative; he tries everything from employing the help of the seagulls to building a rocket ship. None of them work. Disheartened by the process, he heads home along the seashore. Along his way, he comes across a starfish, which satisfies his longing.

The star he ended up holding in his hands looked different than he had intended as he began his journey. It is not so much that he settled for something less than the star he had wished for, but more that he changed his thinking for how his own star could look. Through acceptance of process, we can arrive at the star that fits so perfectly in our hand.

APPRECIATION FOR CREATIVE EXPRESSION

There are certainly challenges in parenting a creative child. Their sense of wonder, love of repetition, and constant desire for more can be overwhelming. Appreciation is the ultimate way to show each other that we value true creative expression.

Honor Impulses

Children are often thought of as impulsive. They move from idea to idea quickly. Impulsivity has developed negative connotations in our society. Children are expected to *control* themselves. Societal expectations for a child's public behavior do not always feel conducive to allowing the process to unfold naturally. There is

"The true harvest of my life is intangible—a little star dust caught, a portion of the rainbow I have clutched."
—Henry David Thoreau

Wonder Words

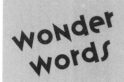

"Shine on."

—Michael Franti

sometimes a degree of difficulty and discomfort for the process and accepting it.

While the ability to calm oneself is certainly a valuable skill, being impulsive is just as important in developing the creative spirit. As we practice creative thinking and problem solving, those impulses will find their own way to balance themselves.

As parents, we can help that along by honoring impulsive moments, allowing and encouraging expression of creative bursts to happen in spontaneous ways. If your child decides that he suddenly needs to tear the paper towel up into tiny little pieces and create a confetti parade or dump out all the Legos™ and mix them with the stones he has just collected on a walk, before reflexively stopping it from happening, ask yourself what harm can be done. As the impulse is arising, come to agreement about how clean up will happen. If your child goes into the experience knowing that you will honor his creative bursts but also have expectations about how they will be handled later, discomfort with the impulsivity can be minimized.

Sometimes honoring impulsivity will mean dropping all plans, stopping everything, and taking a moment to let the creativity bubble.

Let Them Fly

When my son was only a few months old, I learned a song that became part of an "I'm-in-need-of-a-little-TLC" ritual for us. Whether it was my need to sing this to him, his need to hear me sing it, or a little bit of both, we have spent many hours practicing these words together. His favorite verse (which he called the "strings part") went like this,

I can't teach you to fly darlin' one, darlin' one
I can't teach you to fly darlin' one,

But when you cut away the strings and realize you have wings
Will you fly back to me darlin' one?

When children know that their attempts at expression are appreciated and they will always have a loving place to return to, they will be more likely to take those creative risks. We need to provide our children the knowledge of their wings, but also the spirit, passion, and desire to use them.

Creativity is our birthright. We deserve to be able to express ourselves in ways that fulfill us individually. That expression may come in the form of poetry, theatrical renditions, musical compositions, an enormous mess, a new favorite food combination, or an imaginary world. Regardless of the product, we must nurture the creativity, provide opportunities and materials for it to develop, and appreciate how it uniquely emerges to encourage it to blossom throughout life.

Keep wondering, little ones. Hold out your open palms and catch the stars as they fall towards you. Hold onto the stars in your growing hands, but not too tight. May they light the path of your own unique creative journey.

But don't be satisfied with stories, how things
have gone with others. Unfold
your own myth, without complicated explanation,
so everyone will understand the passage,
We have opened you
Start walking toward Shams. Your legs will get heavy
and tired. Then comes a moment
of feeling the wings you have grown,
lifting.

>   —Rumi
>   from the poem "Unfold Your Own Myth"

afterword

Thank you for spending this time with me and for considering how our parenting and learning choices may influence creativity, curiosity, and thinking skills.

I encourage you to try as many of the ideas and products listed here that work for your homes and classrooms. Many of the ideas do not cost more than imagination. For those that do, I would like to recommend that you try to acquire them previously owned. Search flea markets, garage sales, and second-hand stores as they often carry wonderful used (even unopened!) name-brand toys, games, and random items for constructing creative projects. If you are looking for something specific, consider asking friends if you can borrow theirs or posting your request to your local Freecycle (www.freecycle.org) message boards. Visit your local library for resource books, computer programs, audio collections, videos, and even puppets and games. Consider also setting up toy, game, and puzzle swaps, which allow families to temporarily or permanently trade items they are no longer using.

I welcome your feedback, comments, questions, personal stories, and suggestions for future titles in *The Wonder Collection* series. Please feel free to contact me through my website, www.gingercarlson.com.

Happy wondering!

bibliography

Adams, Scott. Personal communication, April 2007.

Armstrong, Thomas. *Multiple Intelligences in the Classroom*. 2nd Ed., Alexandria, Va.: Association for Supervision and Curriculum Development, 2000.

Association of American Pediatrics. *Children's Heath Topics: Media Use*. http://www.aap.org/healthtopics/mediause.cfm.

Baldwin, Rahima Dancy. *You Are Your Child's First Teacher*. Berkeley, CA: Celestials Arts, 2000.

Barks, Coleman, trans. *The Essential Rumi*. New York: HarperCollins, 1995.

Baylor, Byrd. *The Table Where Rich People Sit*. New York: Antheneum, 1994.

Belluck, Pam. "More Schools Offering Prizes for Attendance." New York: *New York Times*, Feb 2006.

Bishop, John. Accent On Success, personal communication. April 2003.

Cameron, Julia. *The Artist's Way*. New York: Tarcher, February 28, 2002.

—. *Walking in this World: The Practical Art of Creativity*. New York: Tarcher, September 29, 2003.

Campaign for a Commercial Free Child, ccfc.org.

Carlson, Ginger. "Totally Smoothie." *VegFamily*, vegfamily.com, April 2004.

—. "Thinking Outside the Recipe." *Mothering Magazine* online, mothering.com, July 2005.

Carlson, Ginger and Harrod, Elisabeth. "Beyond the Sandbox." *HomeAcademy Tribune*, Spring 2005.

Cassidy, Anne. "The Power of Music." *Working Mother*, May 1996.

Cassou, Michele. *Kids Play: Igniting Children's Creativity*. New York: Tarcher, 2004.

Cheung, Mei-Chun, Chan, Agnes S. and Ho, Yim-Chi. "Music Training Improves Verbal but Not Visual Memory: Cross-Sectional and Longitudinal Explorations in Children." The Chinese University of Hong Kong; Neuropsychology, Vol. 17, No. 3.

Child, Julia. www.foodreference.com

Chomsky, Noam. Email communication. March 2007.

Coulter, Dee Joy. "Music and the Making of the Mind." *Early Childhood Connections. The Journal of Music and Movement-Based Learning*, 1995.

"Creative Problem Solving." Muncie, IN: Ball State University, Burris Laboratory School, Teacher's College. http://www.bsu.edu/burris/iwonder/strategies/creativeprob.htm, accessed April 2006.

Csikszentmihaly, Mihaly. *Creativity: Flow and the Psychology of Discovery and Invention*. New York: Harper Perennial, 1998.

—. Dimensions World Broadcasting Network, program 2578.

Cummings, E.E. *I—Six Nonlectures*. Cambridge, Mass.: Harvard University Press, 1953.

Davalos, Sandra. *Making Sense of Art: Sensory-Based Art Activities for Children With Autism, Asperger Syndrome, and Pervasive Developmental Disorders*. Shawnee Mission, KS: Autism Asperger Publishing Company, 1999.

Davidson, Jeff. *The Complete Idiot's Guide to Managing Your Time*. New York: Alpha; 3rd Edition, 2001.

Defty, Jeff. Eugene Public Library. Eugene, Oregon, personal communication. March 2006.

DeGaetano, Gloria & Bander, Kathleen. *Screen Smarts: A Family Guide to Media Literacy*. New York: Houghton Mifflin, April 1996.

Dennison, Paul E. Ph.D. and Gail E. *Brain Gym: Teacher's Edition Revised*. Ventura, CA: Edu-Kinesthetics, Inc. 1994.

—. *Edu-K for Kids*. Ventura, CA: Edu-Kinesthetics, Inc. 1987.

Dodd, Sandra. "Strewing Our Children's Paths." http://sandradodd.com/strewing, accessed January 2006.

Encyclopedia of Creativity. Steven R. Pritzker and Mark A. Runco, eds., San Diego, CA: Academic Press, 1999.

Franti, Michael. "Stay Human (All the Freaky People)." *Stay Human*, Reincarnate Music, 2001.

—. "Crazy Crazy Crazy." *Everyone Deserves Music*, Reincarnate Music, 2003.

Fry, Dawn. "No is Not for Children: Three Principles for Respectful Discipline," http://www.dawntalk.com/NewFiles/No-is-Not.html, accessed February 2006.

Gardner, Howard. *Frames of Mind: The Theory of Multiple Inteligences*. New York: Basic Books, March 1993.

—. *The Unschooled Mind: How Children Think and How Schools Should Teach*. New York: Basic Books March 1993.

Goodkey, Kennedy. "Child's Play: Children's Troubadour Raffi Knows that Having Fun Can Be Hard Work." *Performing Arts and Entertainment in Canada*, 2002.

Gordon, Edwin E. "The Role of Music Aptitude in Early Childhood Music." *Early Childhood Connections: The Journal of Music and Movement-Based Learning*, 1995.

Hanh, Thich Nhat. *Peace is Every Step: The Path of Mindfulness in Everyday Life*. New York: Bantam, 1992.

Hannaford, Carla. *Smart Moves: Why Learning Is Not All in Your Head*. Salt Lake City, Utah: Great River Books, 2005.

Hannah, Gail. *Classroom Spaces and Places: Sixty-Five Projects for Improving Your Class*. Belmont, CA: Fearon Teacher Aids, 1982.

Harrod, Elisabeth. "Questioning Tips to Encourage Creativity and Curiosity." *HomeAcademy Tribune*, 2003.

—. "Child-led Businesses." *HomeAcademy Tribune*, Winter 2004.

—. "Math Manipulatives." *HomeAcademy Tribune*, Spring 2005.

Harrod, Elisabeth and John. Ithaca, New York, personal communication, 2002.

Healy, Jane. *Your Child's Growing Mind: Brain Development and Learning From Birth to Adolescence.* New York: Broadway, 2004.

—. *Endangered Minds: Why Children Don't Think And What We Can Do About It.* New York: Simon and Schuster, 1999.

Hertle, Mark. Howard Hughes Medical Institute, personal communication, 2005.

Jeffers, Oliver. *How to Catch a Star.* New York: HarperCollins Children's Books, Nov. 2006.

Jensen, Eric. *Teaching with the Brain in Mind.* Alexandria, VA: Association for Supervision & Curriculum Development, 2nd edition, 2005.

Joseph Campbell Companion: Reflections on the Art of Living. Dianne K. Osbon, ed. New York: HarperCollins, 1991.

Journal of the American Dietetic Association Online, www.adajournal.org.

Kaufeldt, Martha. *Begin With the Brain: Orchestrating the Learner-Centered Classroom.* Tucson, Ariz.: Zephyr Press, April 1999.

Kennedy, Robert. "Day of Affirmation Address." University of Capetown, South Africa: June 6, 1966. John F. Kennedy Presidential Library and Museum.

Klahr, David. *Exploring Science: The Cognition and Development of Discovery Processes.* Cambridge, MA: MIT Press 2000.

Kohl, MaryAnn F. *The Big Messy Art Book: But Easy to Clean Up.* Beltsville, MD: Gryphon House, 2000.

—. *Mudworks.* Bellingham, WA: Gryphon House, 1989.

Kohn, Alfie, *Unconditional Parenting,* New York: Atria, 2005.

—. "Five Reasons to Stop Saying "Good Job"!" *Young Children,* September 2001.

—. *Punished By Rewards: The Trouble with Gold Stars, Incentive Plans, A's, Praise, and Other Bribes.* Mariner Books, September 1999.

Kraus, Robert. *Leo the Late Bloomer.* New York: HarperTrophy, 1994.

Kristof, Nicholas. "Correspondence/Uncompetitive in Tokyo; In Japan, Nice Guys (And Girls) Finish Together." New York: *New York Times,* April 12, 1998.

Mander, Jerry. *Four Arguments for the Elimination of Television.* New York: Morrow, 1978.

McDade, Carolyn. "Sprit of Life." Surtsey Publishing, 1991 [1981].

McKenzie, Jamie. "Creating Research Programs for an Age of Information." *From Now On, The Educational Technology Journal*, http://www.fno.org/oct97/question.html, Oct. 1997.

McKenzie, Jamie, and Davis, Hilarie Bryce. "Filling the Toolbox: Classroom Strategies to Engender Student Questioning." *From Now On, The Educational Technology Journal*, 1986.

Merriam, Eve. *The Wise Woman and Her Secret*. New York: Simon and Schuster Books for Young Readers, 1991.

Minarik, Else Homelund. *Little Bear's Friend*. New York: HarperTrophy, 1984.

Montessori, Maria. *The Montessori Method*. New York: Schocken Books, 1964.

New Mexico Media Literacy Project, http://www.nmmlp.org.

Orlick, Terry. *The Cooperative Sports and Games Book: Challenge Without Competition*. New York: Pantheon, 1978.

—. *Cooperative Games And Sports: Joyful Activities For Everyone*. Human Kinetics Publishers, 2nd edition, 2006.

—. Email communication, March 2007.

Perelman, Chaim and Olbrechts-Tyteca, Lucie. *The New Rhetoric: A Treatise on Argumentation* John Wilkenson and Purcell Weaver, trans. University of Notre Dame Press, 1969.

Perino, Michelle. personal communication, 2004.

Ralph's World. "Sammy the Dog Has Learned to Play Trombone." *Happy Lemons*, Minty Fresh, 2002.

Ramey, Dr. Gregory, Children's Medical Center, Dayton, Ohio, personal communication. 2003.

Raphael, Raphael. *These Clues*. iUniverse, 2004.

Reps, Paul. *Zen Flesh, Zen Bones, A Collection of Zen & Pre-Zen Writings*. Rutland, VT: C. E. Tuttle Co., 1957.

Rushton, Stephen and Larkin, Elizabeth. "Shaping the Learning Environment: Connecting Developmentally Appropriate Practices to Brain Research." *Early Childhood Education Journal*. Springer Science+Business Media B.V., September 2001.

Sendak, Maurice. *Where the Wild Things Are*. New York: Harper and Row, 1988.

Smith, Charles, A. Kansas State University, email communication, 2004.

"So they Say." *The Scientist*. February 19, 1987.

Soloman, Barbara. "Messing Around." *American Baby*. March 2004.

Striker, Susan. *Young at Art: Teaching Toddlers Self-Expression, Problem-Solving Skills, and an Appreciation for Art*. New York: Owl Books, 2001.

Suzuki, Shin'ichi. *Nurtured by Love: The Classic Approach to Talent Education*. New York: Warner Brothers Publication, 1983.

Sylwester, Robert. "Brain and Media." http://interact.uoregon.edu/MediaLit/mlr/readings/articles/effects.html, accessed March 2006.

Tharp, Twyla. *The Creative Habit*. New York: Simon & Schuster, December 27, 2005.

The Center for a New American Dream, http://newdream.org.

Think Tanks Across Nations: A Comparative Approach. Dianne Stone, Andrew Denham, and Mark Garnett, eds. Manchester: Manchester University Press, 1998.

Thomas, Marlo. "Housework." *Free to Be You and Me*. Performed by Carol Channing, Arista Records, 1983.

Thoreau, Henry David. *Walden: Or Life in the Woods*. Boston: Merry Mount Press, 1936.

Van Horne, Harriet. *Vogue*. 1956.

Wadsworth, Barry J. *Piaget's Theory of Cognitive and Affective Development*, Third Edition. New York: Longman, Inc. 1984.

West, Sherrie and Cox, Amy. *Sand and Water Play: Simple, Creative Activities for Young Children*. Beltsville, MD: Gryphon House, 2001.

Willis, Mariemma and Hodson, Victoria Kindle. *Discover Your Child's Learning Style: Children Learn in Unique Ways*. Rocklin, CA: Prima Lifestyles, 1999.

Wolfe, David. rawfood.com, personal communication. April 2004.

Zappa, Dweezil. Personal communication,1987.

permissions

Permission for quotation use kindly provided by:

Scott Adams, Raffi Cavoukian ("Raffi"), Noam Chomsky, Mihaly Csikszentmihaly, Audrey Flack, Dawn Fry, Ed Gordon, Elisabeth Harrod, Jane Healy, Michelle Perino, Robert Sylwester, Rev. Premanjali and Integral Yoga International for the use of Sri Swami Satchidananda's words, and JUMP Inc. and Roman Vega of Nike for the use of Michael Jordan's words.

Excerpted poems at the beginning of each section from *These Clues* by Raphael Raphael, reprinted with permission from the author.

Excerpt from *Unfold Your Own Myth* by Rumi, reprinted with permission from translator Coleman Barks.

Excerpt from *Peace is Every Step* by Thich Nhat Hanh, reprinted with permission from the author.

Flowers are Red by Harry Chapin, reprinted with permission from Alfred Publishing Co., Inc.

Learning styles checklist from *Discover Your Child's Learning Style* by Mariaemma Willis and Victoria K. Hodson, adapted with permission from the authors.

Excerpt from *Multiple Intelligences in the Classroom* by Thomas Armstrong, reprinted with permission from the author.

Excerpts from *Stay Human* and *Crazy, Crazy, Crazy* by Michael Franti, reprinted with permission from the author and Guerrilla Management.

Excerpt from *The Cooperative Sports and Games Book* by Terry Orlick, reprinted with permission from the author.

Excerpt from *Spirit of Life* by Carolyn McDade, reprinted with permission from the author.

Excerpt from *Leo the Late Bloomer* by Robert Kraus used by permission of HarperCollins Publishers.

PHOTO CREDITS

Page 8: Julie Jackson; Page 12: Cathy Dorrah-Stewart; Page 16: Kimberly Dunn; Page 27: Anissa Thompson; Page 28: Jennifer Haxton; Page 31: Cathy Dorrah-Stewart; Page 40: Anissa Thompson; Page 47: Stock.XCHNG; Page 48: Jennefer Harper; Page 69: Steve Daniels; Page 75: Bryan Güereña; Page 81: Julie Jackson; Page 82: Jennifer Haxton; Page 84: Kim Harris; Page 86: Rebecca Fisher; Page 88: Steve Daniels; Page 94: Leauriy Polk; Page 98: Elisabeth Harrod; Page 100: Mele Allred; Page 106: Jennifer Haxton; Page 110: Julie Jackson; Page 113: Jennifer Haxton; Page 118: Mandi Bussell; Page 122: Valerie Willman; Page 124: Mandi Bussell; Page 125: Ginger Carlson; Page 139: Laura Senes; Page 149: Rebecca Fisher; Page 161: Steve Daniels; Page 183: Cathy Dorrah-Stewart; Page 202: Leauriy Polk; Page 215: Stockxpert; Page 221: Julie Jackson; Page 231: Raphael Raphael

index